Praise for
The Diary of Two Nobodies

'I woke up my wife with shouts of laughter.'
Dominic West

'I read it all night and just adored it. So, so funny
and really rather useful in its sound advice.
What wonderful illustrations, too. Bulging with
humour and talent.'
Susannah Johnston

'I loved it.'
Virginia Ironside

'What heaven. I'm going to read it again.
Hilarious and true and a tiny bit moving.'
Shane Watson

'One of the funniest things I've ever read.'
Henrietta Statham

'So funny and also touching.'
Louise Guinness

'Hilarious.'
Gazette & Herald

'I cried with laughter.'
Joseph1

'A quiet and understated joy.'
Sophia Wood

'I loved reading this book.'
Jelly

'What a fantastic book ... eccentric, charming,
thought-provoking.'
Lisa G.

'Witty, acerbic and thoroughly unpretentious.'
Mrs Mc Small

'Bright, witty and dry.'
Ms R Hinchcliffe

'Found myself laughing out loud on almost
every page.'
P. Hargreaves

'A joy to read.'
John P.

'This is a hilarious and heart-warming book,
a love story.'
Amazon Customer

'A gem of a book.'
Michael JP

'I absolutely loved it.'
Mrs M. G. Powling

'Comforting and amusing.'
Kathryn Gardner

'Interesting and enchanting.'
Mr Fancypants

'All the dry humour and wit of the couple.'
A. Dunne

'Very funny.'
Wilts

'Really funny and interesting.'
Tricia King

'This lovely book is on a par with Alan Bennett.'
Charlotte the harlot

'Never, ever, have I laughed so much.'
Alison Smith

'One of the best books I've ever read.'
Amazon Customer

'Warm and engaging.'
Christine Regan

'Can't stop reading and laughing out loud.'
Baroness Jenkin of Kennington

'Giles and Mary brim with humour,
intelligence and wit.'
Eliza

'It's a genuinely lovely book – intelligent, rye,
perceptive and funny – but ultimately they've
written a love letter to one another and together
prove that everybody is a somebody.'
Jamie Days

'Wonderful and I don't want it to end.'
Tracey Sainsbury

'Giles is an absolute delight, so honest.'
David Todd

'Absolutely nutty.'
Jenna Jeanes

'This is a hilarious journal.'
Idler, selected as Book of the Week

One for Balance

'Thank goodness they're not neighbours of
mine and I don't have to have anything to do with
them in the future.'
Anthony

THE DIARY OF
TWO
NOBODIES

GILES & MARY
WOOD   KILLEN

Virgin Books, an imprint of Ebury Publishing,
20 Vauxhall Bridge Road,
London SW1V 2SA

Virgin Books is part of the Penguin Random House group
of companies whose addresses can be found
at global.penguinrandomhouse.com

Gogglebox is a Studio Lambert production for Channel 4

First published in hardback by Virgin Books in 2017
This paperback edition published by Virgin Books in 2018

www.penguin.co.uk

A CIP catalogue record for this book is available
from the British Library

ISBN 9780753548189

Typeset in India by Integra Software Services Pvt. Ltd, Pondicherry

Printed and bound in Great Britain by Clays Ltd, Elcograf S.p.A.

Penguin Random House is committed to a
sustainable future for our business, our readers
and our planet. This book is made from Forest
Stewardship Council® certified paper.

GILES

To E O Wilson,

Who first inspired my work towards the proactive conservation of amphibians and invertebrates in the quest to restore bioabundance.

Even if, regrettably, at the occasional expense of neglecting my own wife and family.

MARY

To Gug, Karl and Syrah,

Beloved bed blockers who have helped carry the chain.

LIST OF ILLUSTRATIONS BY GILES WOOD

All illustrations - pen and ink on paper.

CONTENTS

PREAMBLE

MARY: My mother always told me to count to ten before flying off the handle. But it's not possible to use this tactic with Giles. Family members and friends know that he actually wants us to fly off the handle following his provocations. We can tell this is so because dimples are the sign that he is happy and they appear in his cheeks as he sees someone ranting in reaction to a bespoke comment which would enrage only that person. And so to the outside observer that person will look hysterical and bad by favourable contrast to gentle Giles with his dimples.

Why does he want to be so annoying? He claims he is suffering from 'classic Middle Child Syndrome'. And that the only way he could get his parents' attention during his childhood was by annoying them.

The other day I found a suitcase of my old diaries in the attic. Inside were thousands of words written in bitterness about Giles's appalling behaviour, and not just the bespoke provocations. From the perspective of twenty years on, they just made me laugh and wonder why on earth I had got so cross at the time.

The treasure trove reminded me of how therapeutic it can be to write things down – a diary is a poor man's psychotherapist. Instead of speaking to the therapist at £100 an hour, and them saying nothing, you pour it all out into your diary and reach the same conclusions without paying.

GILES: Since appearing on *Gogglebox* and suddenly having time to talk to each other, we had begun to remember what we originally liked about each other, and to see how dialogue is the best way to arrive at a peace settlement. With the thirtieth anniversary of our marriage approaching, it was time to expand on this dialogue by beginning another journal, this time with myself as co-author, to take things a step forward by analysing, not just for ourselves, but for the public consumption of the small audience who seem interested in us, anecdotal accounts of the various hurdles life and marriage throws up at a couple in a bid to try to see what, in the dread words of the politicians, lessons can be learned.

In this we are, of course, invading our own privacy but, if it helps other couples to save their own marriages it will be worth it.

MARY: In the meantime, I have recently started, in tandem with my own work diary, which just details appointments, an equivalent rest diary for Giles to prove to him once and for all that he is suffering from a sort of Work Dysmorphia. While he genuinely believes he is working very hard every day on writing and painting and house maintenance, I hope to prove that in fact he is gardening for up to sixty hours a week.

GILES: *Gogglebox* has definitely saved Mary and my marriage. It's a wonderful thing to have a perspective on how you are viewed by other people, i.e. the public, who have seen us on telly, and who, according to the Twittersphere – which neither of us follows but my sister kindly sends me a digest from each week: six positive tweets and one negative (for balance) – keep repeating the phrase 'relationship goals'. I don't know what it means but it seems to be positive. Viewers seem to think it a plus that we are able to finish each other's sentences, for one thing.

Working together by watching telly at the same time, meant that we suddenly no longer lived like two intimate strangers who passed in the night – Mary working from 6 am till 8 pm, then falling asleep slightly drunk at 9 pm; me gardening from 1 pm till 3.30, when I have lunch, and then going to bed at two in the morning after watching vintage horror films like *Basket Case, Carrie* or *The Wicker Man*. These habits meant we had precisely one hour in each other's company per day from 8 to 9 pm, at a time when Mary was shattered after a full day's work and I was at my peak of alertness.

It took public interest in our marriage to make us think about it objectively. Are we actually happy? So

I have agreed to keep a diary – or at least notes and observations of the marriage – as a way of acting as our own management consultants to see what negative patterns recur which could be corrected. Patterns such as Mary gallivanting in London, while I keep the show on the road at home.

The problem with most thirty-year-old marriages is drift. We are told that opposites attract but sometimes our marriage feels like Brexit and Remain. Continental drift is the tendency of tectonic plates to move away from each other. As people grow old they change and their interests diverge, although Mary claims that while she moves with the times I have been 'stranded in the Seventies' and so effectively we are living in parallel universes.

The signs of incompatibility were always there. Mary, upwardly mobile and socially incontinent, while I am downwardly mobile and want to buy a static caravan to reduce costs and restrict my social life to other like-minded worthy folk interested in the pro-active conservation of moths and butterflies and in archaeology. I want to mix with people who can advance my knowledge rather than my social status.

When I first met Mary, we hung out with the Eighties version of the *Made in Chelsea* set, playing court jesters to people who were superior in social rank to ourselves. These were the sort of people who appeared in the Bystander pages of *Tatler* (where Mary had got her first job in journalism). What eventually put me off this set was someone showing me a video of one of the weddings we went to at the time. Although I enjoyed seeing a younger version of myself, I noted I was following Mary obediently around, dressed as a penguin and looking utterly bored and dejected. It was like when you catch a glimpse of yourself in a shop window and you think, 'who on earth is that?'

While Mary's idea of happiness is the sort of conversations which emerge through being a member of a house party of twenty for a week or so, some of the best conversations I've had in the last thirty years have been with a Peugeot mechanic who operates from an agricultural building in a field in Gloucestershire. I found I could easily spend two hours with him putting the world to rights, both of us leaning into the Peugeot estate's bonnet, without any progress on the alternator having been made.

MARY: How come we're still married after thirty years? I believe there's a reason why our generation has more stamina to withstand marital irritation in the short term and wait for the good times to roll around again. We were born and grew up and had already developed our telly-watching habits over decades before the widespread advent of videotapes and DVDs (circa 1985). Tolerance, patience, respectful attention, on the grounds that we will probably see the point if we continue concentrating... those were the values inculcated into us in the days when there was no alternative to 'sitting out' a programme.

As on telly, so in life. Our generation is accustomed to just keeping going through the boring or difficult times while those who've come after us have been programmed, not to 'give it a chance' but instead to fast forward or eject. PROOF: everyone who saw it first time around agrees that the film *Doctor Zhivago* is a masterpiece, yet try showing it to anyone under thirty. They simply don't have the mental stamina to keep watching.

The theory that riding out the bad times and not expecting perma-pleasure will pay off in the long term is borne out by Roger Bamber, partner at the 900-lawyer strong Mills & Reeve. When clients walk in looking to file for divorce, the first thing Bamber does is to try to persuade them not to. Says Bamber, 'Six years down the line, a large percentage of our clients regret their divorce.'

Yet divorce has become something of an epidemic and to me the link with fast forward and eject is obvious. Sticking out the nuisance has much more going for it in the long run.

GILES: I like the idea that, by not divorcing, we are bucking a trend. Moreover, I always say that far too high a premium in our society is based on achieving personal happiness.

APRIL

Wednesday 6th

MARY: I was desperate to go to Marlborough for all sorts of things so my heart sank when, looking out at the glorious view of the Downs from Room Two (see floor plan) I noted that the Volvo was neither in the field nor parked in the road in front of the cottage. Giles had driven somewhere without telling me. And of course, because he doesn't carry a mobile, I couldn't ring to give him a list of what we needed.

GILES: Mary can't drive a car. After 80 lessons over twenty years with three separate instructors she had only mastered the skill of going forward with an instructor beside her in a dual control car. When it came to changing gear she found it challenging, claiming that the 'thinking load' became impossible.

She can ride a bicycle but is wobbly on it and has a lot of minor accidents, for example, with insects flying into her mouth as she is screaming at me to wait for her. I am thinking she might get a moped but we would need to take her to a disused aerodrome to practise riding it. On second thoughts, she might then be mown down by learner drivers who also use these places.

There is a history of moped incompetence in her family. When her aunt Sheila bought a moped for use in her work as a nurse in Belfast in the 1960s, the vehicle was delivered and the garageman demonstrated the starting procedure. But before he had shown her the braking... Sheila, allegedly, got onto it and went round and round the block interminably. Each time she passed the house her family shouted at her to stop but she shouted back that she didn't know how to and had to continue the circuit until she had run out of petrol.

The reason I don't always tell Mary when I'm going into town is that she's a hoarder, and we don't need her to buy any more so-called goods. I don't want to be held up outside an endless series of shops while she goes into a trance, picking things up and then putting them down again like a zombie.

Also, Mary can never find me when she comes out of Waitrose. She says I should carry a mobile so she can contact me and find out where I'm parked, yet I believe that in a small market town she should be able to use her five senses to try to spot the outline of the Volvo parked somewhere on a high street only a quarter of a mile long. I am a great believer in setting initiative tests. As a follower of the Victorian nature writer Richard Jefferies, and a particular admirer of his dystopian novel *After London*, in which an unknown cataclysm causes society to relapse into barbarism, I believe that the innate skills of recognition of basic shapes and patterns should not be allowed to sink into desuetude. Indeed, our survival could depend on them.

Friday 8th

MARY: I have been accused of shopping for things I don't need or 'hoarding', but this is untrue. It's not that I've got too much stuff but that the cottage is too small.

There are three shopping 'opportunities' around here.

Pewsey, although pleasantly one-horse as a town, suffers from a condition we've dubbed Pewsey-itis. None of the shops seem to have the same half-day, for example. Dry-cleaning has to be dropped at the Post Office and the baker charges one pound one pence for a loaf of bread which means the girls behind the counter are constantly having to give out 99 pence in change with all the queue-lengthening time that involves. However, it is intimate with, for example, an electrician who remembers what white goods you own and will mend or change them without a receipt

Devizes is the least near of our shopping opportunities but it yields the most satisfaction for me. Although the town's been over-developed, it has a quaint centre and much more of a feeling of real Wiltshire than has Marlborough. As our old friend

Anne has pointed out, anywhere under a hundred miles from London has a whiff of London *about* it, and Devizes is a good fifteen miles further away than is Marlborough. Devizes has every kind of shop you could hope for, including a stationery shop, a health food shop, a tiny electrical goods shop selling things like two-bar electric fires, an independent chemist, a camera shop selling Kodak film, The Black Swan – a pub on the market square with crackling log fires – antiques and dogs inside it and proper food, to say nothing of a market every Thursday. But for me, the real joy lies in the eleven or more charity shops.

Giles will do anything to prevent me going into the charity shops – for obvious reasons, and who can blame him. But I've always associated shopping with achievement, especially if I've bought what I call a bargain, and he calls 'more stuff for landfill'. He would prefer it if I never was let loose in Devizes, but fortunately for us we are on the panel of an NHS dentist there. The ungreedy saint of a dentist welcomes one of us in there at least once a month so Giles has no option but to drive me.

Giles buys very little on ecological grounds. The one thing he does buy, however, is office furniture. Naturally I don't want horrid grey metal desks or swivel chairs but since we diagnosed his motive for the purchase he has stopped doing it. Basically, he has missed out on office life but has an innate longing for it.

Giles usually hates going to Marlborough because of the spending opportunities in Waitrose, the White Horse Bookshop and the Foxtrot Vintage clothes shop. He feels beleaguered if he sees too many people he knows – for example, former fellow parents at our children's schools – because he finds it hard to be 'pleasant on demand' when he is champing to get back to the garden.

GILES: I'm a busy man. I wanted to quickly slip in to Marlborough's admirable record shop – Sound Knowledge – one of the last remaining off-line means to purchase music, and buy a CD of *Tales from Topographic Oceans* by Yes. I used to own the original copy with artwork by Roger Dean but a former landlady sold my entire record collection in the 1980s at a garage sale. Sound Knowledge is one of the few stores where you can find the album you are looking for just by describing its cover to the owner. A tiny CD, however, is no substitute for being able to pore over the artwork of a 1970s double concept album.

Yes, featuring the eunuchy voice of Jon Lord, produced some of the most self-indulgent music ever to be committed to vinyl, but I have a secret admiration for classically trained, absurdly pompous progressive rock bands, and a particular weakness for Emerson, Lake and Palmer (formerly the Nice), King Crimson – especially the album *Lizard* – and early Genesis – *Foxtrot* and *Selling England by the*

Pound – but mostly when no one else is around. It's funny how music can become a time capsule and send you hurtling back to the less complicated days of its origin. (I mean pre-children basically.)

MAY

Tuesday 3rd

MARY: Another humiliating spectacle today on Pewsey Station. As usual, I'd had to work right up to the last moment. When it was time to leave either I would miss the last morning train to London by packing carefully, or I could simply fill bags with unedited piles of things I *might* need when I got there, including heaps of newsprint to read on the train and discard as I proceed through it.

Of course, it would be a disaster if I arrived in London and found myself without mobile, keys or money, but for some reason I don't seem able to discipline myself to have them in a set position ready for me to grab each time I leave for the train. The inevitable result is that I often find myself serially scattering the contents of the various bags on the station platform as I search to make sure I've got them.

Meanwhile Giles, who doesn't often come to London, turns Quisling, standing at a distance and disloyally rolling his eyes towards the other passengers as I scrabble.

GILES: As Mary, bent double on Pewsey Station, scatters the contents of her bags onto the platform and rummages through an assortment of biro tops, buttons and receipts, I recall the image of the peasant in the Van Gogh drawing *Peasant Woman Gleaning Ears of Corn*.

Mary has too much stuff. And on the theme of Van Gogh, I believe the only way to live in a cottage is with just the bare minimum of necessary items a table, two chairs, and an axe for cutting wood. Nothing else.

MARY: I too crave Spartan Van Gogh-style interiors. I'm never happier than when staying in a hotel with a manageable amount of stuff (and some empty surfaces to tip that stuff onto for sorting). But the reality is that Giles and I both work at home, and that although he is minimal to a self-sabotaging degree, I'm a writer with an archive of magazines I've written in. As a freelancer, your accountant requires you to keep all your bank statements and general financial papers for at least six years in case you are investigated. And what about packaging? You must think ahead to the moment when your computer or other electrical product goes wrong and the courier comes to take it back to be serviced.

BAGWOMANING ON PEWSEY STATION

'Please retain all packaging for this purpose,' say the instructions.

I also need to hoard clothes as I wait for them to come into fashion again. From an early age, I experienced the gratification of finding in our attic in Northern Ireland such mothball-guarded treasures as 1950s cocktail dresses, 1960s Pucci print sundresses with zips up the front and 1970s Forbidden Fruit mirrored hippy skirts.

Transported to my own Wiltshire attic these have been seized upon by our daughters, named Fleur and Rosie. No, of course those are not their real names but, to avoid invading their privacy, we'll refer to them as such. Giles can't see the expense spared by not having bought these clothes for huge sums from a vintage shop. He can only see clutter.

Oh dear – I also have memorabilia – old family papers and things like my doctor great grandfather's leather and mahogany medical examination couch, which give me a three-dimensional link with the pillars of Presbyterian probity which made up most of my antecedents. There is no room for it in the cottage but neither can I bring myself to send it to a dump or to an auction at which it might raise two pounds.

As I said, it's not really that I've got too much stuff. Rather that the cottage is too small, and Giles should be helping me sort and tidy the attic to make room for more stuff, but of course he's too busy.

Friday 6th

MARY: Looking down at the garden from Room Two I saw Giles going to and fro through the gate and into the road with a watering can... then I looked out of the front window and saw him inexplicably pouring the water into a trench in the road.

'Have you gone mad?' I called.

'I was watering the road for the house martins so they can repair their nests. It's so dry and dusty there's no mud around otherwise. You say I don't work. Well if this isn't worthwhile work, I don't know what is.'

Saturday 21st

MARY: Cyril and Ursula have come to stay. Giles and I are certainly compatible when it comes to our taste in people. We've always loved the same ones. We find that we gravitate towards eccentrics, bossy personalities and the opinionated, and we both seem to enjoy obeying the orders of the domineering. Cyril and Ursula, however, are Lib Dem voters and fall into none of the above categories. We've just known them for thirty-five years and our children grew up with theirs.

Sharing tastes in people is good for many reasons, one of which is because such people have a vested interest in your staying together and don't try to undermine your partnership. We don't have guests nearly often enough for my needs – but on the rare

GILES WATERING THE ROAD

occasions when Giles nods his assent, the prospect of someone coming incentivises us to tidy the cottage, set log fires a-going – in our telly-watching room or, for bigger parties, in Room One. This is our biggest room whose purpose has never yet been clearly designated. Is it a work room, a dining room or Giles's art studio? It's not clear, so we call it Room One.

And then, behind Giles's back as it is un-eco, I tackle the bathroom stains with the lethal but super-effective Spirits of Salt.

I've always found that other presences in the cottage provide welcome human buffers between me and Giles. In terms of a peace-broking initiative it's helpful to see these independent observers (who harbour no bitterness about missing furniture, believed burnt on a bonfire, or broken seventeenth century Rummer glasses from Ireland which 'just jumped out of the machine' into which they should never have gone in the first place) roaring with laughter at Giles's jokes, appreciating his cooking and his *recherché* collection of worked flints from the Stone Age, which he has picked up on the Downs.

Giles served fishcakes which he'd made himself. After supper Cyril and I did a jigsaw on the card table in front of the crackler (cottage-speak for log fire) and we all watched a DVD of *Andrei Rublev* by Andrei Tarkovsky which, at 205 minutes, is, like marriage, another test of endurance and requires quite a bit of mental stamina. Few of our other friends would be interested.

Scrabbling about on the wooden floors in the background were our two dogs, Phoebe, our Tibetan Spaniel who is a girl but who we always refer to as 'he' – it's a tradition in this neck of the Wiltshire woods to refer to all dogs as 'he', whether female or not – and Pip, the West Highland Terrier belonging to Cyril and Ursula, who actually is a he. Phoebe and

Pip have known each other all their lives and always try to mate, even though Pip has been neutered. Ursula and I love to see the happy look on Phoebe's panting face, though Giles and Cyril invariably tell the dogs off.

Sunday 22nd

GILES: As well as too many possessions, Mary also has too many friends. Fortunately, fewer of them seem to want to come and stay these days. I've often thought of harnessing the data in the Visitor's Book to produce a bar chart of what would prove to be diminishing guest numbers over the years, but Mary says this would be a waste of my talent, which would be better put to use on getting on with one of my many outstanding painting commissions.

Why have the numbers gone down? I don't believe it's because I've alienated people, as Mary sometimes speculates, it's simply the fact that the conditions in the cottage are no longer good enough for people of our own age group. While economically most of our contemporaries have saved and prospered over the years, Mary and I have flatlined. Cyril and Ursula are among the few grown-up couples happy to brave the 'Pointy Room'. This is the downstairs guest room off the sitting room, which has a vaulted twenty-foot-high ceiling. The children called it the Pointy Room because of its pointy ceiling.

We always provide clean white Irish linen on the eighteenth-century French bed (an Irish heirloom of Mary's), but the room – three out of four of whose walls are outside walls, thinly insulated and clad with larchlap decking – is chilly to the extent that in winter it can even be almost windy in there. During bad weather, the whole Pointy Room turns into a wind instrument resembling a giant Aeolian harp as the draughts gust through it starting on one note and rising a full six tones before falling again.

The Pointy Room was originally used as a log store by our next-door neighbour, in the days when all the cottages in the terrace of five had a so-called easement meaning they were all allowed a right of way through each other's back yards. No one had put up dividing hedges because there was no individual mindset. The occupants of the terrace all worked at the Manor Farm which eschewed brutalist farm machinery and had traditional toilers in the field, right up until 1985.

Bert, our next-door neighbour, had become a taxi driver when the farm was eventually mechanised. One of ten sons, Bert's father used to keep order by boxing the boys' ears, as was the norm in agricultural families. Who has even heard of a parent boxing someone's ears today? It would certainly be illegal and social services would step in. Ear boxing has gone the same way as black eyes and scabs on knees. Using raw steaks to cure black eyes was a great feature of the *Dandy* comics of our youth. You never see them these days. The result was that Bert, born in 1928, was quite deaf and quite aggressive. His constant companion through the lanes and fields was his German Shepherd, Holly, trained up as an attack dog, who only Bert could control. He frequently asked our guests, who might have gone for a walk around the lanes, to 'Stop right thur!' This was not addressed to his own dog but to the person walking. He would then make a great palaver of putting the slavering beast onto a chain.

Bert had been used to storing his logs in that then-empty Pointy Room which had an open outside door leading into the communal garden. Bert knew his rights and announced that he would hang onto them even after we had bought the cottage and moved in.

But Bert was a betting man, and when the would-be vendor of our cottage turned up at Bert's one night with a wodge of one hundred one-pound notes (which were legal tender in 1988) and offered them to Bert if he would sign a form relinquishing his right to store the logs there, Bert leapt at the chance and we were able to convert the log store, into our guest bedroom.

MARY: It can be chilly in there but, once installed in the bed, guests invariably attest to having had a sound night's sleep. I think it's because it's cosy being in a room off another room where you can hear a television still going and a log fire crackling and, of course, once the television is turned off there is nothing but silence from the gloriously empty countryside around the cottage, or 'Little House on the Prairie' as Giles, a member of the soil association, refers to it.

GILES: Otherwise guests stay in the Slit, also known as Room Three. This is a tiny room only slighter bigger than a sleeper on a Scottish train We named the room the Slit after an anecdote of Mary's mother.

This involved the outing of a couple, a very old woman and a very young man, who no one in Mary's family could believe could be romantically involved and yet when, in front of overnight guests, they disappeared together into a very small bedroom, described by Mary's mother as 'a slit of a room', to spend the night, the family had to conclude that they were indeed a couple.

Monday 23rd

GILES: I enjoyed the visit of Cyril and Ursula. Usually, however, I prefer to have a single person to stay in the cottage. As a house guest, a single person is a much more manageable commodity. As Mary says, guests tend to act as human buffers between us and, in fact, they do make me behave better than I would otherwise.

If there are more than two guests, I tend to start annoying them. My grandmother said I was born to annoy. A boy whose surname was Arkle, like the horse, shared a study with me at school and I used to do elaborate spiral shaped designs in felt pen on the leaves of his tropical houseplants. Arkle was intrigued by the manifestations which he attributed to an infinitesimally small exotic pest which must be lurking on the underside of the leaves of the plant. To my satisfaction he wasted many hours with a magnifying glass trying to locate the mythical bug. It all came to a head one day when I went too far and drew a smiley face on one leaf.

I believe it all dates back to Middle Child Syndrome and wanting to get attention. In childhood at least I could always be sure of being snapped at even if I couldn't get any other attention.

In the 1990s I owned a spring-loaded, ex-World War shell cartridge which dispensed one-pound coins and which I used, on occasions, to partially pay my Jungian psychoanalyst when I visited him in North London. I did this first because I felt it would highlight how difficult it was for me to raise the money for the sessions, and secondly to see if I could get a rise out of him – which would, of course, be unprofessional of him. I considered the few occasions when he did rise to be personal triumphs. Once, having finished the session and left the room, I popped my head back round the door and asked him if he had anything planned for the weekend. He snapped back, 'That's an inappropriate question. You're not a colleague of mine. You're an analysand.'

And once when I asked him, while writing a cheque to top up the coins I had dispensed, to remind me of the spelling of his name. 'It's Newman. There's only one way to spell it and you've asked me about four times already!' These I considered the high points of our relationship. Now, looking back, I realise that what could have been a unique journey of self-exploration was probably one of the wrong channels into which to divert my abilities to annoy.

The coin dispenser was more appropriately used in the days when I used to accept pheasant shooting invitations – despite the fact that all the other so-called guns were around a foot taller than me. I liked to tip the keeper using the one-pound dispenser kit, which I often had to struggle with, while the other 'gentlemen' were discreetly palming him a stiff note.

I know I am annoying to Mary when I stay up late for no real reason. Why do I stay up till 2 am watching B horror movies? For example, *The Hills Have Eyes*, Wes Craven's movie, shot on location in the badlands of Dakota, about cannibalistic mutants from nuclear experiments who have devolved into a subspecies who prey on innocent campers and specialise in grabbing their feet from concealed mineshafts and yanking them down inside.

My reasoning is that I feel it's my duty to watch, almost in the role of censor, so I can warn my children not to. Although I do have standards and would never watch any of the *Human Centipede* franchise...

Wednesday 25th

GILES: Before *Gogglebox*, both Mary and I believed ourselves to be so busy that when disputes arose, there wasn't time to let one have the chance to put their point across while the other one listened. As a consequence, we tended to both speak at the same time.

Some years ago, Mary made a double appointment for me with our excellent GP. Anti-depressants were then, as now, all the rage, and one of our friends (whose whole family had been chemically coshed) insisted that I too needed to be medicated. Moreover, Mary's older friend Marigold, a professional psychotherapist, said my distinct lack of artistic, financial and even social ambition were markers to signal that I was suffering from depression.

When the time came for the appointment I refused to go unless Mary came too. In the surgery I announced that it wasn't I who was in need of medical treatment it was instead clearly Mary. The excellent GP gleaned that we would do well to have ten (free) sessions of marital counselling provided by and at the surgery at tax payers' expense. We took him up on the offer.

We enjoyed the sessions very much... at least I did, because (as with the Jungian analyst) I managed to make the counsellor lose her cool with me.

Mary had complained that I followed our nanny around the house too much to check on what she was doing. On one memorable occasion, while she was making the children's tea in our tiny galley kitchen off Room Four, another room without precise designation but on whose table I was sorting chestnuts, the children ran through from the sitting room to urge Melly to come and watch J K Rowling on television.

Melly duly hurried through and I allegedly caused resentment by taking the opportunity to quickly follow her into the sitting room with a duster, saying, 'That reminds me Melly. The screen needs a dust and polish. Perhaps you could do that while you're watching.'

Mary had taken exception to this interference. The counsellor asked me what had been my motivation. I explained that I identified strongly with Hudson, the butler in *Upstairs, Downstairs*, memorably played by Gordon Jackson, who believed there was a natural social order. The Bellamys were on the rung above Hudson and the kitchen maids were technically on the rung below him. But Hudson somehow pulled off the brilliant feat of being neither upstairs nor downstairs but 'on the landing' so to speak.

Since I believed that, although in the outside world I too was 'on the landing', within the cottage, I surmised, I was at the top of the class pecking-order. I therefore considered it was incumbent on me to ensure that Melly worked as hard as possible.

The counsellor snapped, 'I hope you are being facetious because if you seriously believe in any natural social orders in the late twentieth century, then these sessions are at an end.'

I consider it was very unprofessional of her to have risen to my bait.

But the sessions taught us a valuable lesson regarding the resolution of inter-marital disputes. This is that a couple will make no progress if they both speak at the same time. Mary and I found that just being able to express our grudges without the other interrupting was therapy in its own right. Ever since, during arguments, we will use an oven timer to take turns to allow each other five uninterrupted minutes for putting our individual point across. One holds forth whilst the other one listens although Mary has, on occasion, required me to wear a gag while it's her turn to speak.

Friday 27th

MARY: Marital concessions: I've made huge progress re throwing things out since my friend Louise gave me a copy of *The Life-Changing Magic of Tidying* by the Japanese writer Marie Kondo. Essentially, Kondo's message is that you should process one category of clutter at a time. Let's say you start with cardigans. Collect all the cardigans in the house from wherever you have stored them. Place them all together in a pile. View them. When you see how many you have you will find it so much easier to differentiate between the ones which 'spark joy' in you and the excess which, realistically, you will probably never wear again and, in fact, feel indifferent towards. You make a pile for the charity shop, the dump, or to give away to friends.

You then move on to skirts, dresses, coats, hats, even underwear. Then you start going through books, kitchen equipment, cosmetics and so on.

The theory is that you are eventually left with a house which only contains things which you definitely love. Using this method I have managed to dispose of at least three car-boots full of 'grot', yet Giles is blind to the improvements.

The clutter dysmorphia from which he suffers, i.e., miscalculating the amount of clutter there is, was probably triggered in the first place by the incident when our shoe designer friend Emma Hope moved house and gave me about 30 pairs of her own lightly worn Emma Hope shoes. Equivalent value today to the three females of the household all with size 39 feet to around £10,000, but Giles could only view the treasure trove as 'clutter'.

Then there was the time when our friend India got divorced. She and I were having lunch in London when she announced that she was going up to Scotland the next day, to clear her wardrobe and take all the contents to a charity shop in Dundee.

'Can you tell me which shop and its address?' I enquired.

'Why?' asked India.

'Because I'll be going up there and standing outside the shop the next morning ready to walk in and buy everything. When else would I be able to afford such quality stuff?'

We laughed, knowing it wouldn't happen, but a few days later a delivery van pulled up outside and a courier came staggering towards the cottage with three washing-machine-sized boxes full of clothes – the entire former wardrobe of superkind India.

The contents have stood me and our daughters in great stead over the last ten years but instead of being grateful for the savings, Giles felt suffocated.

'I'll only allow you to take these into the cottage, Mary, if there is a simultaneous stream of clothes going out. So I'm going to stand here with these empty boxes until you've filled each one of them with an equivalent amount that I can take to the dump.'

'Why are you robbing us of this moment of peak happiness?' we three females screamed.

Looking back, I can see why Giles might have felt threatened by size of the influx. What was annoying though, was the Basil Fawlty-type mania and urgency with which he wanted to see the same amount of clothes going out.

GILES: In my view, the most destructive thing a 'friend' can do to us is to gift us another plethora of their own unwanted clothes. They turn the cottage into an obstacle course.

The one exception to the hoarding disaster is that Mary unearthed from the attic a video called

No Going Back: Janique. This documentary about
an English woman, Jane, who bought an island on
Nicaragua's mosquito coast for £150,000, named it
Janique, a combination of 'Jane' and 'Mustique', and
moved her children and husband there, is one of the
most interesting things I've ever seen. It's a grotesque
inversion of the dream of buying a desert island, in a
tale that would have provided suitable material for
Joseph Conrad. Others agree so much so there is an
online forum about it but, it soon came to be viewed
as one of the most 'unsuitable' programmes ever
broadcast, and so it has been deleted from Channel
4's catch up site. It has achieved cult status amongst
cottage visitors who watch this videotape (we have
one of the last households in Britain with a video
machine) with mouths agape.

JUNE

Monday 6th

MARY: So Giles and I are off to Florence on Wednesday to attend the wedding of Gug, who is almost a family member. Gug weighs not an ounce more than nine stone and Giles, who is a little envious of Gug because our daughters and I love him so much, refers to him as Mr Puniverse.

It's almost exactly ten years since we first met Gug one Saturday lunchtime, following which he came to work for me for 'two days' but swiftly made himself indispensable.

It was David Smith, the Head of English at a local school, who introduced us. David had arranged an end-of-term barbeque in his garden so that those sixth formers who wanted to go into journalism (in those days it was still a possibility that there might be a job available), could meet some people with hands-on experience of the trade. David had rounded up ten local practitioners including Giles and myself, Cyril and Urşula (who then lived locally as their children were at school in Marlborough), the then-top inter-viewer of the *Sunday Telegraph* and the then-*Times* parliamentary correspondent.

I remembered seeing this young figure, who resem-bled nothing so much as Hergé's Tintin, standing on the edge of a conversational cluster which contained Cyril and the parliamentary correspondent of *The Times*. I noted that Tintin was silent but was laughing at all the right jokes.

I introduced myself to him and Tintin/Gug replied that actually he and I had spoken on the phone during the time he had worked at the *Spectator* as a part-time receptionist while he was a student at UCL, and when he had been put in charge of compiling the *Spectator Book of Wit and Wisdom*. Gug had sent me the entries he'd selected to represent my own wit and wisdom from my 'Dear Mary' problem page, for my approval.

'I remember!' I cried. 'Because the examples of my wit and wisdom you chose were the very ones I would have chosen myself.'

Now I'd actually met this person who was so clearly exactly on my wavelength it went through my mind that I should try to extract more journalistic services from him.

It emerged that he had had to leave London since he had now graduated from UCL and none of his student friends wanted to go on paying rent for their shared flat in London. As he couldn't afford to live alone he had been forced to give up his job at the

Spectator and boomerang back to his GP in Oxford father's house.

It was only June so he now had time on his hands before starting his new term on a one year teachers' training course in September, so I opportunistically asked Gug would he like to do a couple of days' work for me.

'I'll pay you the minimum wage,' I said. 'And you'll have free delicious food cooked by Giles.'

'What would you want me to do?' asked Gug, smiling.

'I don't know exactly…' I pondered, '… just generally obey me.'

When he burst out laughing and said, 'all right' I realised here was a soul mate.

Gug arrived (late – he always has been late ever since). He didn't need to obey me; he took it on himself to walk the dog, tutor the (then) children, mend bicycle tyres, go shopping, force me to go on walks and to Weight Watchers, read aloud to me and the children, and generally be just good company. The French writer Alexandre Dumas, fils, said, 'The chain of marriage is so heavy that it takes two to bear it, sometimes three.' Gug's eventual residence in the cottage was this theory borne out in practice and shown to work.

Obviously there was no romantic relationship between me and Gug, but he served as a human buffer between me and Giles during those ten years in which he worked for us – sporadically, but often enough – and as his career advanced, sometimes

I worked for him. He got on with what Giles called 'his own little career' in journalism, into which he was successfully springboarded through his association with us. And then he bought 'his own little cottage' four miles away.

Until Gug was snatched from us by his own inevitable marriage, his presence helped ours. Not just because he is never bad tempered. He was able to run down to whatever room Giles was shouting from to find out what he wanted, and the sight of this other human standing in front of him would shock Giles out of his gardening trance and cause him to be more reasonable in whatever request or demand he was about to make of me.

Gug was the third person carrying the chain of our marriage. Then there were more Gugs, a series of bed blockers, as Giles uncharitably referred to them, in the form of the three young people who were at the start of their careers at that stage and one by one stepped into the Gug void. There was Karl, Gug Two, now head of scholars at an Oxford prep school; there was George, Gug Three, now running a Scottish stately home in the Borders. And there was once Syrah, a female Gug, who was by far the most efficient of all the people who worked for me. She virtually tied me to my chair and made me process one bit of paper at a time. No job was too menial for Syrah, once a saddo spinster who spent her weekends wandering on Salisbury Plain with a scotch egg and a flask of whisky in her pocket, now a happily married mother of two with a global audience for her botanical artworks. The Gugs came singly and they could be found sleeping either in the Slit or the Pointy Room.

Giles referred to them as the bed blockers, but secretly he enjoyed their company for reasons earlier outlined. They would find him very funny, they liked his food – particularly his full English breakfasts with black pudding – they admired the way he grew and chopped his own logs and most pertinently they would go to see what he wanted when he called me from another room while I was sitting down with a load of newsprint or other paperwork on my lap. The trouble is that the vintage Gugs have *all* got their own little lives now; they are too successful to want to come and skivvy for us.

GILES: One of the reasons why Mary liked the Gugs was that they were all good drinkers, while I can only process three units per day. If I have more, I develop a condition called Fish Eye where my eyes change shape and I can't stop yawning, the yawns often culminating in a high-pitched yelp.

Being bed blockers was only a rite of passage, though, I always knew that one day they would leave us with Empty Nest Syndrome – just as Fleur and Rosie have.

MARY: Some say the clue to Giles's sometimes unreasonable behaviour is simply that he has never worked in an office. It is working in an office, or

A BED BLOCKER IN ROOM THREE

at least in a workplace scenario with colleagues, which civilises us. We can behave badly at home where we can assume the fellow occupants will forgive us because they love us, but our colleagues can't be assumed to be even fond of us and therefore we can't behave badly in the workplace. People talk about the School of Life, but Giles has never attended that school.

'There were three people in the marriage and it was a little bit crowded,' Princess Diana famously told Martin Bashir. But, in my opinion, had the third person been no romantic threat, she would have welcomed his or her presence.

As our friend Tom points out, 'Not everyone can afford to hire a human buffer as you hired the Gugs. But it's certainly true that the presence of a third party in a household usually makes a couple behave in a more civilised manner – in most households this role is taken by a child.'

'Or,' as Giles points out, 'in the past, a servant.'

Now we no longer have the Gugs nor our children in the household, we have to find ways of getting along without them. This was why it was so useful to our marriage when *Gogglebox* came along.

While we wait for each programme to begin, we end up chatting to each other for about three hours a week in total. Some of our chatter eventually gets broadcast and we have been amazed to hear from Giles's sister's, who monitors Twitter, that people have found something we said funny. How interesting that other people have found our chit chat funny when we thought of it as irritable backbiting. It certainly gives you a new perspective on your life.

But also, because both of us are so busy, we had got out of the habit of discussing things and so now these scheduled chats became our opportunity to revive our 'parliament', which used to take place in the Volvo in the days as we drove the children to school when we would discuss forthcoming business every morning.

Gradually we realised we were enjoying the *Gogglebox* 'preambles' – indeed they became an essential cog in the wheels of the marriage because, as with the counsellor all those years ago, we had to take it in turns to speak. And then we realised that we had a huge amount in common, although, as Alain de Botton has pointed out, you are barking up the wrong tree if you are searching for a partner who is compatible with you. What you need to be focussing on is honing the skill of negotiating the inevitable incompatibilities between you and your partner.

But to get back to Gug One, I think the very best thing about his influence on the domestic happiness quotient within the cottage was that Gug himself is a happy person and laughter comes easily to him. He laughed almost continuously – but not sycophantically. He laughed at the right jokes.

It made us think that we were funny. This boosted our morale. Moreover, if this clever, sympathetic young observer found our irritated backchat hilarious rather than harrowing – then maybe our marriage wasn't as bad as it sounded to us.

But the truth is that man and woman were not designed to spend twenty-four hours a day in each other's company. What underpins most successful marriages is the knowledge that irritation, if it arises, will only be short-lived since you will soon have an eight-hour break, at least, from the perpetrator because he or she will have gone *out to work* while you can bask in the blissful mental privacy of having the dwelling to yourself and thereby build up the reserves of good nature which will allow you to greet your partner's return from the coal face with genuine enthusiasm.

Tuesday 7th

MARY: Giles is still complaining bitterly about 'having' to go 'abroad' to Gug's wedding. 'I know you are over-subscribed with guests,' he told Gug, 'so I'd like to help you out. I'll volunteer to give up my place to make room for someone who might be chippy they haven't been asked.'

'But Giles!' cried Gug. 'You're practically my father! I couldn't possibly not have you there.'

Giles has been acting Basil Fawlty re the travel arrangements. Quite frankly his company has been intolerable for the last three days, especially without Gug to dissipate the tension.

GILES: I believe that trips abroad should be planned and run like a military operation and what I find difficult to grasp in the modern age is that so many things are left to happen spontaneously.

For example, my inability to book flights online, check-in online etcetera meant that I had left Mary in charge of organising our trip to Italy for the wedding of Gug, a family friend (we leave tomorrow) and as a result I suffered from anxiety because she had only booked three nights' accommodation in Florence for a six-night trip!

If left to me to arrange the trip I would've tried to go to Thomas Cook, purchased travellers cheques, purchased a new money belt, and worried constantly about inoculations and how to avoid foreign pickpockets. I like everything planned beforehand and not arranged on the hoof.

MARY: These days, if twenty-something 'children' are involved, you can't plan trips abroad like a military operation. No arrangements can be set in stone since the Young now change plans right up till the last moment and I didn't want to book rooms if we weren't going to use them. Re the boarding cards: Giles is the only one who has to have his printed out. This wastes endless time because, of course, all the printers in the village, as is the nature of printers, are broken. The rest of us can have electronic boarding cards sent to the wallets in our iPhones.

Wednesday 8th

GILES: Mary found it annoying that I went missing for forty minutes on the way through Departures at Stansted and didn't answer my (analogue) mobile. The problem was that after my luggage was forensically searched I repacked the mobile in my cabin baggage instead of my pocket so I couldn't hear it ringing.

But why did I try to conceal a jumbo-sized deodorant spray in my luggage in the first place, knowing that it would be spotted and, of course, thrown away?

One: to see if the security system worked – my window on the world is the *Daily Mail* and I worry that low-cost airlines may be cutting back on safety or maintenance. Two: I must enjoy being searched. Three: I think I have a thing about bossy women in uniforms because at the back of my mind I may believe I deserve to be punished. For that reason I gave my searcher just enough cheek to annoy her by asking, 'Is there any reason why the searching has to proceed at such a glacial pace?' but not enough to get myself arrested.

On the whole, I see myself as a classic type of English man: 50 per cent Basil Fawlty, 20 per cent Alan Partridge, 20 per cent Mr Bean (especially when travelling) and only ten per cent David Niven. I think the future is female because men's inability to adapt to change and to multitask renders us like so many defeated generals with our heads in our hands. At my public school I was educated to be a leader of men and yet my family consists entirely of women and I have never worked in an office or in an organisation. Hence there is a feeling of redundancy – except on Thursday evenings when I swing into action by putting out the relevant recycling bins for Friday mornings.

Friday 10th

GILES: This morning, Mary and I find ourselves tucked away in a musty corner of a quiet café located in the northern quarter of the Piazza della Repubblica. Over café Americanos we both stared in silence at the passers-by. My newly acquired anorak, a Berghaus 1 shell-hooded lightweight model, which would provide the most impermeable protection from the rain but not from the heat, is duly rested on the back of my wooden chair.

Mary finds anoraks very un-aesthetic and, when we're at home, she resents the presence of so many on the various chair-backs of our tiny cottage. She also complains of the 'noise' of the anoraks while I am wearing them. However, living with ever-increasing climate chaos, the quest for the perfect anorak will, as far as I am concerned, continue. I very much admire Chris Packham's choices of immaculate anoraks and would love to know the brand name of Ray Mears' green anorak. Or is it brown?

MARY: Giles is colour blind which causes additional hiccoughs in life, for example when he is referring to the 'white' telephone, what he means is the yellow one, or meconium yellow as he likes to call it – even though it isn't meconium yellow, he has been fascinated by the word meconium since we had our first baby.

GILES: As we look out onto the Piazza, I realise that almost everyone in the street is transfixed by their iPhones. I can see that an iPhone is a very good prop to make it seem as though you are connected to the larger world, but the fact is that I'm not involved in this larger world. I don't even know what an app is, what Instagram is or a Snapchat, and this makes me feel isolated at times. The times like this, when I have left the cottage.

The problem is that I'm a slow learner, like I'm a slow reader and have slow delivery. It doesn't mean I'm not intelligent, but it means that no one in this fast-moving world has got time to teach me how to do things at a slow and logical pace. Recently, for example, I had collected a series of newspaper cuttings about an unfolding drama concerning my godson, who had been charged with masterminding a crime abroad He was innocent but risked spending a life sentence in jail if this could not be proved. I was pleased with the fact that we had been fastidious in collecting every story as the drama unfolded over weeks, and I'd been looking forward to showing the bundle of cuttings to our younger daughter (Rosie), when she came home on one of her rare (detox) visits, and I would finally be able to get her attention for a moment while her mobile was charging.

I couldn't understand why she showed no interest. 'What you don't realise, Daddy,' she said, 'is that my generation has read all the news before you have because it comes up on Facebook. And yes, it's amazing what's happened to Harry, but we see at least three amazing Snapchat Stories on our phones each day.'

MARY: Even though I am much more digitally aware than Giles I was unfamiliar with Snapchat Stories. Rosie showed me a few examples – they are short films of her friends water-skiing, another one hang gliding over an empty desert, a third one on stage in a nightclub belting out a song as a pop-up member of a band to an audience of a thousand… No wonder she has 'amazement fatigue' – she can barely process the reams of astonishing digital data that come at her every single day.

GILES: The idea that our own daughter might be suffering from 'amazement fatigue' is depressing. She says I must be the only man in 2016 not to carry a 'smart' phone. I do own a pay-as-you-go mobile but, even when I do carry it, it is usually switched off.

We are living in an era of accelerated, technological change and it's only a matter of time before humans are subsumed by technology as predicted by Futurologists in a phenomenon called The Singularity.

You can already see evidence of this by witnessing what happens when the till in the village garage shop breaks down and immediately a queue of angry customers begins to snake around the forecourt. These days there is no alternative to the chip and pin. I'm proud to be resisting the dependency on machines and to be able to describe myself as an analogue man in a digital age.

But I have asked myself why I have no appetite to ride the techno wave?

Missing the wave has been a very important theme in my life and not just metaphorically. There was the time when I sat in the sea in Polzeath for a full two hours waiting for the perfect wave to ride in on but the surf finally stopped and I never rode one. It was hesitation. The same hesitation that led me to turn down offers of exhibitions – 'Am I ready for it? Perhaps you should put me into a group show' – and commissions from important collectors by asking for example, 'I'm not sure it's the right time of year for me to do any painting in a room which might appear to have a very cold light.'

And the one important book deal. 'There seem to be so many books out there already. Wouldn't it be a blessing if I were not to add to the mountain? There are too many writers chasing too few readers as it is...'

When the offer to appear on *Gogglebox* came in, I was only five years away from the age my father had died at. The 'contents page' of my life was looking a bit thin and I thought the time for hesitation was over.

Besides, I had a vague memory of once appearing on Radio 4's *Woman's Hour* on an item about hypochondriacs. I remember saying that on the rare occasions when I took public transport I staved off minor infections by continuously chewing extra strong mints and exhaling more than inhaling, and I discussed the time I grazed the roof of my mouth on an upturned crisp, which had put me out of action, conversation-wise, for at least thirty-six hours.

I remembered I had enjoyed the attention; first of entering the studio and having people fussing around me, then of having my views taken seriously enough for someone to bother recording them, and finally I enjoyed getting feedback from friends who had heard the broadcast.

Sunday 12th

MARY: After watching dear Gug tie the knot in the English church in Florence and attending his reception in a hired house above the city, we returned to our hotel room. I was exultant, but as Giles lolled back on the hotel bed I sensed he was settling in for some negorrhoea.

I've recently eschewed the oven timer method of solving arguments. Instead I employ new technology. I've found that for more gritty major disagreements, it can be illuminating to set the Voice Memos feature of my iPhone going and record the arguments so later I can type them up and print them out so we can assess which one of us has been unreasonable. In anticipation of his putting a dampener on the glorious proceedings which had taken place, I determined not to rise but instead just to record. The taping was not covert. Giles allowed me to do it but, as one does, he quickly forgot the tape was rolling.

Later on playback, I heard myself gushing about the triumph of the wedding and Giles retorting that it was 'a triumph of style anyway' and that the young groom had exhibited very little composure. Gug had sobbed as he took his vows. Giles griped that he must have been watching rather too many Grayson Perry documentaries attacking the macho culture.

GILES: In my generation there was a thing called the stiff upper lip and we were taught not to show our emotions in public. One should at least be able to get through something like a marriage ceremony with a reasonable degree of decorum and not blubber away like Kate Winslett at the Oscars. I was fully expecting him to clap his hands and say 'gather!' It's usually the woman who shows elements of emotion and the man should be robotic.

MARY: I had to point out that men were different in his young day. The stiff upper lip was the norm because those were the days before all the oestrogen had entered the water supply through women being on the Pill and on HRT. Oestrogen is an exquisitely potent hormone which can't be filtered out. Result: feminised fish and frogs and men, and ball-breaking women like the Williams sisters.

The carping continued with Giles complaining that for the same price as two nights in Florence we could have had a week in the Canary Islands and me saying yes but we got to bond with 200 really nice people in a short but intensive scenario, then Giles said that we might have 'over-reached ourselves socially' and I retorted that this was inverse snobbery – why shouldn't the classes interact? Giles said he felt it would be more natural for us to interact with solicitors, town planners, metallurgists and...

'Dental hygienists?' I suggested.

'No,' pondered Giles, 'perhaps dentists and principals of agricultural colleges...'

Giles went on searching for something negative about the marriage he could 'harvest' from the experience. Without success. But why did he want to harvest something?

'Why, you might ask, did Gug bother grooming us all those years and buying a cottage in the Vale of Pewsey if he was just going to get married and leave us?'

Mystery solved. Giles was just as sad as the rest of us to be losing Gug as a bed blocker. His 'grief' was being expressed through carping. The mystery would never have been solved without dialogue.

Friday 24th

GILES: We voted Remain but when I got up this morning I saw the Leavers had got four percent more votes, but I had no one to discuss it with. Mary has been staying in Austria with our neighbour Christof who has a 'second home' there. I was asked too but it rained every day the last time I was there. Mary says this was an illogical reason not to go and I mustn't blame Christof for the weather which is beyond his control and that it's 'such fun' inside his Austrian house in any case.

But she has much more social stamina than I and enjoys after dinner games and attempting to dance the Polka while wearing silly hats. In any case, she seems happy to go and stay in house parties without her own husband.

I ask myself what are husbands for these days? No longer needed as escorts to houseparties, neither are we needed as breadwinners, map-readers, soldiers – not even as builders. In Jamaica I saw women hod-carriers. Apparently they are favoured over the males on that island because they don't need to stop for ganga breaks. It's a trend that will be heading this way soon.

At least I am still useful for drain unblocking, checking the salt levels in the dishwasher and removing the rosemary stalks from the filter.

Monday 27th

MARY: I got back from Austria and Giles confronted me as usual by saying that I was lucky he had stayed behind because he had kept the show on the road by killing slugs, etcetera. Frankly I would much rather he had just come to Austria than stayed behind to kill slugs. Did he really want me to stay behind? No, he likes me to go to things and report back to him, partly because it means he can 'enjoy' whatever I've been to by proxy but without having had to make any social effort.

He asks, 'What are husbands for these days?' he might as well ask 'What are wives for?'

Things have moved on since the Seventies, the decade where Giles is stuck. Those were the days when an Englishman's home was his castle, ditto the Englishwoman's home. She had eight to ten hours of blissful mental privacy per day while her husband was out at work and she was well incentivised to behave herself when the breadwinner came home.

Of course, everything was neat and tidy and meals were on the table and the exquisitely groomed wife would suck up to the man when he came home (bringing the bacon). After all, he would be in bed and fast asleep three hours later.

I would love to spend all day cleaning and tidying and cooking for Giles coming home after a hard day's work but the fact is that he 'works' at home and I 'work' at home as well. Which one of us should suck up to the other and which do the housework?

I used to feel there was no room in marriage for both partners to have a career. Were I to devote myself to Giles as a full-time aide, making his breakfast, lunch and dinner – even though he is a far better cook than I am – doing all the cleaning and tidying and the admin and all the buying the paints and washing the brushes, and the work that an agent might do such as soliciting clients and then recording who had bought what, then maybe miracles could occur. Indeed, he is more talented as an artist than I am as a writer. Or, if he were to sublimate himself into my career and to the resolution of my anxieties, perhaps we too could achieve miracles.

However, because I have to write two columns a week, hold down a job as a PR to a Jamaican businessman and do the admin for the adult children, we need the immediate cash flow.

That is why it was so good when *Gogglebox* came along to help us both to achieve something together.

Tuesday 28th

GILES: There has been too much going on in the garden for me to tackle the house. During our absence in Florence, Phoebe the dog was looked after by our former nanny Melly and they did not come to the cottage, but what never ceases to amaze me is the amount of hoover matter which seems to generate itself in a room that no one has even been into for a week. It is as though there has been a Glastonbury Festival of nanoparticles partying in the house while you have been away. I am interested in all matter at floor level, particularly the whimsical galaxies of dust and fluff under beds, and will happily hoover, especially enjoying using the crevice nozzle, and mop, leaving Mary free to tackle anything above floor level including ceilings. Between us we should be able to act as a team to 'clean up' like Jack Spratt and his wife to cover all bases, but somehow this doesn't happen.

When I am in cleaning mode I do find it satisfying to see how black the liquid in the bucket goes. I am very keen on 1970s cleaning agents like Flash and Ajax powder (increasingly hard to find), which always seems to produce a pail of water and a mop which are completely black, whatever I have been cleaning, as if we have been living in the most polluted inner-city areas next to a coal mine rather than in a rustic Arcadian idyll.

I like nothing more than to end the chore by throwing the pail of water violently onto the former lawn from a great height. When Mary challenges me about this I advise her that nature is very good at dealing with small quantities of pollution.

Tonight we are expecting a visit from Harry, a single man who is helping Mary with one of her literary projects. As previously noted, we tend to work together in harmony when we are having people to stay and we make an effort to make it nice for them.

Other people, no matter how fastidiously they keep their own domestic quarters, seem to love the cottage. But following the visit of a nine-year-old child who described it as 'the house with all the notices', Mary has become self-conscious about the number of warnings I've had to put up and says that lately I have put up too many, e.g., in the sitting room, 'Please do not ask to borrow a book as refusal may offend'. In the kitchen, 'Shut the freezer door'; in Room Two, 'Do not open this window' and in the Pointy Room 'No Love-making'. Usually this only applies to Cyril and Ursula.

I love a bossy notice. The folk in the big house have erected a sign from yesteryear on their field gate advising that, 'Failure to secure and fasten the gate will result in a fine not exceeding one shilling'.

It's only partly a joke. I suspect that they actually mean it. Strange words that you never use in conversation can be employed in bossy signs, i.e., 'Please 'refrain' from smoking in this food preparation area.' Mealy-mouthed words like 'rectified', suddenly come alive. As in 'Please check your change as mistakes cannot afterwards be 'rectified'.

I am currently working on the wording of a new bossy notice for our library to deter book thieves. Just as in the old days folk would think nothing of using your telephone if you were away, or stealing a bottle of wine from a party on the basis that 'I might have drunk it anyway but I had a hangover' so some people become light-fingered when surrounded by an interesting collection of 'borrowable' books. Max Bellows, at the time a Marlborough schoolboy, was one such offender who borrowed my rare book about hallucinogenic mushrooms. It took me two years to get it back from his bedroom on the top floor of a mansion outside Oxford! And involved much subterfuge and mental gnawing and resentment.

'We do not lend books. Therefore please do not ask, as a refusal may cause offence' is almost there, but not quite. I would like to get the word 'desist' in somewhere.

My mother, however, is less bothered by the notices. For her, the levels of cleanliness fall below the 'minimum standards' which were decreed when she attended Winkfield, the finishing school for a certain generation.

But even though guests know the cottage is not overly clean, they know the beds will be clean, the so-called surfaces of the kitchen and bathroom and the vitreous wares. But no one should attempt to run their fingers over the top of picture frames.

Why is everybody else's house so immaculate? Even on telly the houses for sale on property programmes always look like show homes

In our case, as our garden is organic it means we do have more insects, spiders' webs etcetera than other cottages. One thing I would never use is a Vapona unit and we are deeply suspicious of microwaves.

One of our key bonding moments occurred when Mary was expecting our second child in 1993 and we attended the Cornference (Crop Circle Conference) in Glastonbury, Somerset, along with legions of other credulous New Agers, old hippies and readers of *The Cerealogist* – the limited circulation magazine edited by the late John Michell.

We live only three fields away from the classic formation of a crop circle that Led Zeppelin used on an album cover; the field was a magnet for Japanese tourists over many summers. Glastonbury was too far to drive home from after the lectures (which virtually confirmed an imminent invasion of little green men) so we had booked a B&B to sleep in afterwards so as not to miss out on this seminal event.

We managed to get the last room in Glastonbury. When we arrived at the house at about nine thirty that night, the room we were shown into was painted a brilliant, marzipan white over anaglypta wallpaper. There was not a fingerprint or a stain to be seen anywhere.

The double bed, whose bedlinen (polyester) was almost crackling with biological detergented cleanliness, was almost as big as the room itself

There were no fewer than three hermetically scaled windows with Vapona units belching out toxins, plus, in the ensuite plastic bathroom, a lavatory freshener almost as big as the lavatory bowl itself.

The room was as spotless as an operating theatre but we knew immediately that we could not spend a night in it.

Mary and I looked at each other and my normally dormant masculine protective instinct came into play as the hormones were clearly making her vulnerable. 'Eraserhead,' she whispered.

It was a code word we both understood.

No room had ever so actively replicated the atmosphere of that 1980s film by David Lynch, which, we both agreed, was the closest thing we had experienced in waking life to being in a nightmare.

I took the owner aside and told him that Mary was pregnant and had come over queer. I offered to settle up there and then but he allowed us to go without paying as he had a cancellation customer waiting to take up the 'suite' if we didn't. As we drove away I told Mary that we would go straight ahead and spend six times as much on a poncey hotel we knew half way home. I treated her. We have rarely been happier. It was the thought of having escaped the Vapona units that swung it.

Thursday 30th

MARY: Living twenty-four-seven with the same person means that inevitably patience will be overtested from time to time.

This morning, our neighbour Rosemary called to collect an envelope she had dropped off a few days ago asking for a donation towards a charity. I headed for the parking coins jam jar but found it empty.

'Just a moment Rosemary,' I said. I opened the door of Room Four and called, 'Giles! Have you seen the pile of coins that I collected for parking and that were in this jam jar yesterday?' I knew Giles was in the telly room. He had heard the latch of the front door being clicked open and had scarpered to hide in there to avoid being 'emotionally drained' by having to be pleasant to whoever might be coming in.

Since there was no reply I burst my way into the telly room. Rosemary, who was standing behind me in Room Four, must have been alarmed to hear me suddenly scream 'Stop nodding!'

As it turned out, Giles had decided to hide my collection of about twelve pounds in parking coins on the grounds that 'you should never leave money lying about to tempt thieves', but in the short term he couldn't remember where he'd put it. Giles reacts badly to 'unreasonable workloads'. Being 'put on the spot' like this, 'without notice' and being asked where coins are when somebody has dropped in unexpectedly had sent him into Churchill-dog nodding mode.

This is where he expresses confusion by nodding as though he has developed a neurological disease which is manifested by nodding. I know it's not funny but it's something he's started doing.

'Stop NODDING!' I will scream. And his mother warns him, 'You had better be careful Giles – or one day, sooner than you think, you'll find you can't stop doing it.'

Yet Giles insists that by rehearsing doing the nodding deliberately now, he will be in a better position to control the reflexes in old age when it may well have become involuntary.

JULY

Friday 1st

MARY: 'Hugo has diverticulitis,' said Giles this morning. How did he know? He doesn't answer the phone and no one had come to the cottage for the last 36 hours. He looked uncomfortable when I put him on the spot asking for proof.

'All right, he hasn't got it,' he confessed. 'But his cleaner has it.'

'Oh Giles, I can't cope with your Hatrollalia.'

GILES: My mother and I both talk on occasion through our hats – a condition Mary, with her medical background (her father was a doctor), has dubbed Hatrolallia. In a famous example, my mother responded to my brother's news that he had bought tickets to watch Sir Roger Norrington conduct Berlioz's *Harold in Italy* at the Royal Albert Hall by saying, 'Don't be silly, darling. *Harold* is only ever performed at the Festival Hall. It's a tradition.'

'How extraordinary!' said Pip. 'I could have sworn it was the Albert Hall.' Reaching there and then into his wallet for the tickets, he showed the words 'Royal Albert Hall' to my mother who retorted, 'Well don't jump down my throat, darling! I just said the first thing that entered my head.'

Mary was particularly annoyed by me one day, nearly thirty years ago, when, in an example of my own Hatrolallia, she heard me tell Rebecca, a journalist/writer friend that she, Mary, was now doubly incontinent following the birth of Fleur, our first daughter.

MARY: Giles loves negative news, so I could pick up from the enthusiastic tone of his voice that something must have gone wrong for Rebecca. (See Giles Wood's 'Encyclopaedia of Mishaps and Miseries', his mental compendium of things that have gone wrong for friends and family – even nightmares that they had forty years ago all dutifully recorded.)

Then I heard him say, 'Well that's awful – but Mary's actually doubly incontinent now, since she gave birth.'

Not only was I not doubly incontinent, but even if I had have been, it would not be an ideal image to have circulating about someone (me) who was at that time editor of the supposedly glamorous Bystander social pages of *Tatler* magazine.

Naturally I snatched the receiver and told Rebecca it wasn't true and forced Giles to admit the same.

Afterwards Giles told me off for 'barracking' him when he was on the phone. 'I was just trying to cheer

Rebecca up,' he explained. 'She was just telling me she had to have an operation after her baby was born and she couldn't stop peeing. She's written an article about it in *Cosmopolitan* called "Sex after Stitches". I felt sorry for her so I thought if I told her you were doubly incontinent it would make her feel better. But then you have to go and spoil what was probably the only piece of good news she'd had all day. Poor Rebecca!'

GILES: By the way, when I told Rebecca that Mary was doubly incontinent, I can remember now why I said it. I had just heard the phrase 'doubly incontinent' for the first time and wanted to try it out.

MARY: Giles has never had the ability to see ahead to the consequences of the Hatrolallia remarks he makes.

There was a similar incident many years ago when Giles was working as a painter and decorator for a now world-famous actor, then appearing in one of his first major stage roles in *Another Country*. A minxy friend of ours was secretly having an affair with this then-aspiring thespian. 'What do you think of him?' she asked Giles who, of course, had no idea that Minx and he were romantically linked.

'He seems a bit of a cipher,' Giles had replied, beaming. Giles told me later that he'd just heard the word 'cipher' for the first time and, though he wasn't quite sure what it meant, he wanted to 'try it out'.

Little did he know that our minxy friend would go straight to the actor, and report the comment back to him with devastating effect. We all know, of course, how supersensitive and insecure an actor can be and the upshot was that the actor, who did know what cipher meant, went into a deep decline.

Giles has since speculated, however, that it might have been the very charge of being a cipher which spurred the actor on to such great heights, since directly after the blow to his ego, his career made a meteoric take off. He became a world class actor by means of his thorough and total immersion of the roles that he chose. For this Giles takes all the credit.

Tuesday 4th

MARY: Our cul-de-sac village at the foot of the Downs was, until thirty years ago, rarely penetrated by strangers, since everyone living here, except for the two spinsters in the Old Rectory, worked for the farmer who lived in the Manor Farm. It was a feudal village with all the front doors painted the same shade of red to signal allegiance to the Farm. The only people who came through the village would be itinerant knife grinders or people selling clothes pegs. The sight of anyone else would excite suspicion.

Eventually, in 1985, the venerable farmer died at the age of 98 and new farming practices came into play. The human workers were inevitably trumped by machines and sprayed chemicals and had to take up other professions. One villager became a chimney sweep, one a postman, one a bus driver and two went onto the bins.

But old traditions die hard and vigilance is still exercised when strangers come to the village. Hence, during an attempted afternoon power nap in Room Two, I was surprised to hear a dialogue between two unfamiliar voices going on under the bedroom window for around ten minutes. Eventually, I gave up and took off my eye mask. Looking out, I could see Giles himself, leaning on the gate leading into our field, talking with a wayfaring youth who lived here as a boy but now under the lee of the local hill fort of Martinsell. He was roaming through the local lanes to exercise a dodgy knee. But why was Giles mimicking the young man's Wiltshire yokel accent?

GILES: I have just explained to Mary that my own father (who had a fireplace manufacturing business in Stoke on Trent) used to talk to his slabbers in a thick Potteries accent. It was their own patois and so he modified his voice to talk to them. This would be a different voice to the one he would use when meeting other Company Directors in the Potteries.

MARY: I said to Giles that was all very well but Daniel Crowbourne has seen Giles on television and knows he doesn't speak with a Wiltshire accent. Giles retorted that I can't talk because I have permanently changed my own Irish accent and this is absolutely true. I have had to change it for the simple reason that when I first came from Northern Ireland I could make no conversational progress as everyone imitated everything I said back to me in a sing-song whine rising up at the end of the sentence.

But at least I stick to the same accent now instead of varying it depending on to whom I'm talking. There are certain words I can never pronounce un-Irishly though. These include iron, path, bath, shower, scoop, route or boost. To say nothing of Prague and Cannes.

Thursday 7th

MARY: If I'm reading quietly in Room Two and Giles, coming in from the garden, doesn't realise I'm there, I can overhear him using the telephone in the room below, Room One. He doesn't answer calls on the grounds that he doesn't like surprises but he does make them.

Around this time of year, he will usually ring up his sister, his brother and his mother to be negative about the fact that they are 'missing' each other's gardens.

'Your garden and Ann Wood's garden both peak in June, but June's over,' I hear him say to his sister who lives near Oxford, 'and I've been too busy to see it.

'Pip Wood's garden peaks in the second week of July but, although Mary's only just got back from Austria, she's off gallivanting again and she's forcing me to go with her to Mull next week. There may be a slot in August for you to come here, but you'll be in Wales for most of the month and my garden will be over by then. Because of global warming everything comes on at once.

'It makes a nonsense of our gardening lives if Mary is always going to force us onto this relentless social treadmill so that we all miss each other's peak moments. I have absolutely no desire to trek to Mull but Mary has press-ganged me into it.'

This was an example of Seancespeak. I knew he was looking forward to going to Mull. I'd taken the precaution, that morning of recording, on my mobile phone voice memos app, our 'Parliament' as we thrashed through the pros and cons of him joining the house party on the island and he had concluded that he would love to go.

Seancespeak is when Giles says things he couldn't possibly mean. It's when he channels other people – not himself, as he imagines how these other people might respond to something that has happened. I first coined the phrase when I heard him declare 'You can't beat a battery chicken for value and they taste just as good as free range' and was dumbfounded until I suddenly realised he was channelling my stepfather, Eric, from beyond the grave.

So, when he said he had absolutely no desire to go to Mull, he was in fact channelling his friend Gerry, who would have had no desire to go there as there's no signal in the house and not enough retail outlets nearby. I lift the extension and tell his sister Jackie that, if she's interested, I'll send her the voice memo by email so she can listen for herself to the reasonings which helped him to arrive THIS MORNING at the decision that he would absolutely love to go to Mull.

Jackie is deeply loyal to Giles and so she laughed uncomfortably. She always feels she should side with him.

Friday 15th

GILES: Mary has roped me in to another house party for twenty. My desire to meet real, genuine people – people interested in cetaceans (porpoises, whales and dolphins) – struck me forcibly on the way to this house party in Mull when I came across, on the ferry, an earnest-looking, but fascinating group who were excitedly discussing sightings of the rare basking shark. They were going to camp on a remote penin- sula of the island to study these gentle giants (not the *Jaws* variety) and I got into a conversation with them about whether or not we should all dispose of our fleeces. I had just read an article about how when fleeces are washed they release toxic microbeads and they were very interested, and began picking self-consciously at their uniform of choice – a fleece. I felt that I could easily spend a week happily chat- ting to them.

On arrival at the lodge I immediately went fishing with one of the oldest members of the house party and was amazed to find he could not identify one of the most common birds in Britain – a heron – despite being a Scottish landowner himself. How do I meet other ecologists in general? Or deep ecologists in particular?

<u>Monday 18th</u>

MARY: I flew up with John and Veronica without Giles, who only decided to come at the last minute and had to travel by train. To me it is pure bliss to spend a week under the same roof as about eighteen other pleasant people with an age span between three months and seventy. There is always someone to chat to, and every breakfast and dinner is cooked while we make our own picnics for outdoor lunches each day.

I don't know how Giles gets away with it but his popularity seems undimmed by the fact that he sneaked away last night after dinner instead of playing the Book Game. When I came upstairs he asked me how the 'charades' had gone. When I told him it was the Book Game and not charades he said, 'Oh no! Why didn't you come up and get me then? If I'd known it was the Book Game I'd have been happy to join in. It's just charades and Scottish reeling that I can't stand.'

As a matter of fact, I had gone up to the bedroom to quickly get something and Giles hadn't been in it.

'But you weren't even here when I came up,' I said.

THE HERON.

HERON (AFTER THOMAS BEWICK)

'No,' he replied. 'I'd popped out to look for bats in the gloaming. But you should have made more of an effort to find me.'

Friday 29th

GILES: Mary is away in London for a few days, so it falls on me to keep the show on the road and, being colour blind with no specific training about different fabrics, I tend to dive into the laundry cupboard which is situated – against common sense – in the kitchen near foodstuffs. Conditions which, if replicated in an Indian restaurant would force its closure. After some rummaging I mix and match the dirty washing and set the load going in a batter wash.

What comes out of the machine is sometimes grey and tighter fitting than erstwhile. But my philosophy is that even if some of the fabrics come to grief by being washed at the wrong temperature, we have too many clothes cluttering up the cottage anyway so it will do no harm to cull some of them. And at least we will have made progress.

There's nothing worse than a cupboard with a lingering load full of clothes which have been 'basted' into. It was long ago explained to me by our older friend Anne, with whom we often stay in Kensington, the difference between honest sweat and nervous sweat.

'The former can be triggered from an act of exertion such as chopping wood, the latter might be triggered by shame,' she tittered. Or indeed an official letter from Wiltshire Police, following an incident of entrapment, informing me that I was doing 38 mph in a 30 mph limit exiting Hungerford for the M4, and I would need to decide between penalty points or a time-consuming speed awareness course near Newbury.

At the risk of being indelicate, or offending readers, this letter may have triggered a fight-or-flight

reaction complete with nervous perspiration redo-
lent of the kitchens of a kebab house in the Uxbridge
Road, Shepherd's Bush (no offence), but why does the
body have such a ready supply of 'tincture of onion
and inferior badgerburger' and would a change of
diet fix it? I have watched *Cowspiracy*, the documentary credited with converting so many of the young
into vegans and vegetarians and I can hardly call
myself an environmentalist without giving up meat,
but I haven't.

The most compelling argument for me would
be if giving up meat permitted one to ditch the
deodorant... But, are vegetarians free of body odour?
I don't think so. The dread word 'sprouty' springs to
mind when one thinks of the air quality in a room
with even one vegetarian inside it.

There was a red-haired boy at my prep school
in North Wales called McDonald who swallowed
the entire dormitory's supply of Haliborange (five
bottles) in one go. He liked the sweetness of them
in those days before sweets were so widely available
to children. He had to go to the san for observation.
Apart from turning orange, all his freckles joined up
together and he smelt of tangerines for two weeks
thereafter, which serves him right. One of those
bottles was mine.

Of Mary's many faults, doner kebab-type bodily
emanations are not one of them. So, obviously, being
a considerate sort of a fellow, I like to frequently
change my shirts, even though this leads to a charge

from Mary that I have been producing 'vexatious' quantities of ironing for her to tackle.

<u>Sunday 31st</u>

MARY: I am cross with Giles when he produces too much laundry because otherwise, when there is a manageable quantity of ironing to do, I enjoy it. My sister, who has more common sense than me once asked baldly, 'Could Giles not wear a boiler suit rather than ordinary clothes?' And then, 'And why is the washing machine constantly churning with table clothes, napkins and chair covers? Could you not just stop spilling things?'

I love ironing for the warm feeling of competence as I observe a visible transformation from chaos to order and all of it executed by my own hand.

The truth is that I would be far happier cleaning all day than doing the sort of complicated jobs requiring thinking that I have got myself involved in. Earning the money to keep the cottage over our heads comes first in the pecking order of time parcel distribution. Writing-work is time consuming because what's easy to read is hard to write.

I enjoy ironing not just for the heat and the instant result, as well as for the obvious metaphor. The pile of things needing to be ironed is altered from crumpled to smooth. I can make a miniature stack worthy of an Irish linen store and, as Giles has observed, 'the process of ironing settles the molecules of the mind into flat layers rather than chaotic ones'. It is so enjoyable I have to stagger the ironing and only allow myself one piece of ironing for every five pieces of grot filing.

Time was when we had a nanny and we also had Meg Vardens to do the ironing. How did we afford it? These days I have to do it myself. At first I resented the chore but then I moved the ironing board up to the only reliably hot room in the cottage – Room Two, our own bedroom and sometime office, which has the best view. Positioned in there looking out over the Downs with, in sequence, Nick Ferrari and James O'Brien of LBC booming out of the radio as I iron I am rarely happier. But only if I have the time.

And lately Giles, who has too much time on his hands, has developed a phobia about his personal 'freshness'. Correction: I believe he is pretending to have developed such a phobia as he so enjoys seeing me toiling away on his behalf that he is deliberately using more clothes than he needs. I call it vexatious laundry.

One of the problems with a cottage of this size and with the opportunity for water outlet pipes being confined to only one side of the room-deep cottage is that we have literally no space empty in which we could put a tumble dryer. At least we no longer drape our laundry over the banisters and radiators (which broke a few years ago and we haven't had the money to replace them). Now we have a pop up electric clothes horse from Lakeland which does the job. But lately we have also read alarming news which may explain why our asthmatic daughter has developed an allergy to the cottage. Apparently airborne moulds thrive on indoor drying laundry.

AUGUST

Wednesday 10th

MARY: Giles can watch an episode of *University Challenge* and get seventeen questions right. But he can also be inexplicably dim-witted from time to time. We call it Variable Intelligence Disorder. And I'm not the only one to have noticed this.

Today, Giles and his mother were pruning roses together in the garden, below the window. I am ironing in the room above them, Room Two.

'Mary won't be able to come,' I heard him say. 'She's taken on too much.'

You've taken on too little, I thought to myself.

'No. I'll come up on my own to Wales, Mum,' Giles continued. 'Mary works nine-eleven. She won't be able to get the time off...'

'It's twenty-four-seven Giles. Not nine-eleven. People work twenty-four-seven!' said Ann Wood.

'Well how did I get the idea it was nine-eleven? I'm sure it's nine-eleven, Mum. Do you want to check – on the internet? You could Google it.'

The other day I handed him a hand-written thank you letter I had written to Veronica and John to thank them for having asked us to Mull. We were in the television room and I saw him read the first page with enthusiasm. Then he cried, 'Don't be silly, Mary. You can't end a letter like this in the middle of a sentence without even signing off.'

'I haven't done,' I seethed. 'Turn the page over.'

'Ah, there it is,' said Giles. 'Well, why didn't you tell me it was a two pager?'

Without Gug's sympathetic presence in the house I find the VID hard to take at times. It's as if I'm going mad. And I'm particularly upset about the fact that Giles has started having his tongue out.

I laughed the first time he did it – it was like the way slower witted children used to read when we were at school. But now he's doing it all the time and I don't know if he's just trying to annoy me or whether he's got something actually wrong with him, but when I scream 'Put your tongue in!' he now replies, 'Please let me have it out, Nutty. Now that I've started doing it, I find it's so much more comfortable to have it poking out. Why don't you try it?'

GILES: One of the stupidest things I've done was joining Amazon Prime (for 'free' next day delivery) because I wanted a parcel to be delivered the next day. Mary wasn't there when I was punching in the instructions with my sausage fingers. I had no idea that if I failed to cancel it, it would cost me £79 a year until the day I die.

I have never used it since and I've no idea if they are still taking the money out of my account because Mary always hides my bank statements before I've had a chance to look at them. And then she sends them to the accountant so that's the last I ever see of them. It's her way of keeping me in the dark and infantilising me.

One of the earliest examples of my having Variable Intelligence Disorder was at prep school when we were made to do an intelligence test. One of the questions was 'which weighs more – a ton of bricks or a ton of feathers?' *Easy*, I thought. Naturally the bricks got my vote and secured my entry into that exclusive club DENSA, the polar opposite of MENSA. No one in an official capacity had ever tried to deceive me before, and this experience gave me a lifelong fear of entrapment.

When I was entrapped in a motoring offence by a policeman lurking in a depopulated leafy area in Hungerford where the 30 mph limit suddenly turns into forty, it happened because I was just starting to put my foot down to enjoy the freedom of the roads. I was doing thirty-eight as I approached the forty sign. As anyone would, I opted to attend a speed awareness course rather than receive points on my licence (clean as a whistle despite Mary's protestations that I drive dangerously).

I hated the course and I've no time for those folk who claim to have really enjoyed it and who talk about it for months afterwards with all the zealotry of converts. I found out that the fellow who ran my course also moonlights as the proprietor of two dodgy nursing homes. That says it all.

Thursday 11

GILES: We are leaving our money troubles behind and heading to North Wales to stay with my mother, but Mary has packed a sheath of mortgage papers to sort through as she seems to be addicted to busyness.

When Mary was organising the mortgage for this cottage, she was looking for something in her basket and systematically unloaded one item after another onto the mahogany veneer antique bureau separating her and the mortgage broker. I remember she told me how his face gradually morphed into a mask of impatience and irritation, and he snapped, 'If you take one more item out of your bag I'll give you a smack' (those were the days before 'abuse' was recognised as a source of income). His professional cool was severely tested and to this day I still suspect that the mortgage deal Mary negotiated was the wrong sort.

MARY: I've got too much to do as usual but sometimes if you bring paperwork with you and sort it out in other people's homes, it's easier to deal with – partly because other houses tend to have empty surfaces whereas the cottage tends to have none.

It's always worth going to Anglesey if you get the chance. People come in packages and Giles's package includes his mother. She is enthusiastic about all manner of wholesome things: windy coastal walks, dogs, flowers, building dens and making fairy cakes – which she used to help her grandchildren to make, all three of them wearing linen aprons and then tidying up nicely afterwards, before licking the bowl. She has a wood-burning stove which makes her house overlooking the Menai Straits and Snowdonia toasty all the way through and a third of it is light-filled because, as a former Victorian peach house, it's made largely of iron and glass. She has a lovely musical voice, knows all about plant and wildlife, and has a sharp and well-stocked brain.

GILES: Mum was once a Brown Owl in the days when the middle classes would volunteer and do good. She's the sort of woman who knows where things like thermometers and nail scissors are without having to overturn the house. She believes that a woman's place is in the home.

MARY: The trouble is that she also seems to believe a man's place is in the home as well. Or in Giles's case, the garden. The two of them spend hours congratulating each other on the progress the other one has made.

'Well at least Mum appreciates me,' Giles has just said accusingly. 'She says I've done really well to have made my own runner-bean wigwam from my own coppiced hazel.'

'Yes – but at the expense of not having completed your painting commission.'

'But a mature garden adds thousands to a property, Mary so it's money earned in kind.'

'But we're not selling.'

'We may have to at the rate you're spending,' he says from a doorway. He always likes to stand in a doorway during an argument because it is almost out of earshot and he likes to ratchet up the tension when we are having a disagreement. It's called passive aggression.

GILES: This is an exit strategy. A sharp exit strategy as in the Carlsberg ads. It allows me to duck into another room and lock the door behind me. Or even jump out of a window. As a woman from Northern Ireland, Mary is fully capable of adopting the ways of violence that characterised the Troubles.

MARY: Of course, I'm never properly violent but I like to reach for some kind of spray product like Windolene when we have these rows. I come towards him spraying a fine mist in the hope of triggering an asthma attack to get my revenge. Naturally, he runs away. Once I locked him into Room One when he had done something really awful about which I felt so strongly that I continued to spray Pledge through the keyhole until the plastic bottle ran dry.

GILES: Our daughter even suggested that I ring the help group Mankind for battered husbands yet I read in the Mail today an article telling me that the word 'mankind' is now politically incorrect and no longer allowed.

When the children were small, Mary and I once went on a skiing holiday. We joined a large party who had hired a chalet in Wengen. It was to celebrate the sixtieth birthday of one of my father's oldest friends, Gill Waterstoner. Mary can't even walk in ski boots but she was just recovering from Legionnaires' disease and Gill thought that the rest would be good for her. She could go back to bed after breakfast every morning and then come up the mountain to join us for lunch.

Meanwhile, my mother came to stay in the cottage to look after the girls then aged five and eleven. We found remarkable accelerated learning on our return. One child was singing French songs in a French accent, the other putting her bowl into the machine after she had eaten out of it. What was Granny's secret? She attended to the task in hand.

She did not read an article and talk on a mobile while simultaneously putting a child to bed. In exchange, she had the child's full attention. It was then that I realised we needed Mum's help nine-eleven. Imagine if there were four hands picking caterpillars off brassicas rather than two. And there were jobs like step sweeping which only got done when she came to stay. Then it dawned on me: perhaps that's why she lives in Anglesey.

Saturday 13th

MARY: It's a heat wave on Anglesey and we are sunbathing on Red Wharf Bay, winner of a Clean Eurobeach award.

Many New Age visualisation techniques for inducing mental calm involve imagining yourself lying on a beach. This never works for me because I can't think of a beach experience which didn't involve anxiety. Especially during the children's childhood.

Heroic as men can be at responding to danger (toddlers or small dogs being washed out to sea) or to theft, they seem to lack the imaginative faculty to anticipate such likely results of inalertness. So a woman can't risk closing her eyes on a beach unless another woman on the next lounger can be inveigled into keeping watch.

GILES: It's not surprising Mary can't relax on a beach as she brings so much stuff with her and then spends ages sorting through her bag looking for the various items. Moreover, I never know why she doesn't carry everything in a sensible, waterproof, zip-up bag instead of a sisal African shopping basket with all its potential for the contents to spill out.

MARY: It's funny how all men seem to consider a loaded woman's bag or basket to be a symbol of neurosis rather than a repository of useful items which they themselves will be plundering in the fullness of time – e.g., water, towels, suncream, bite cream, reading matter, tissues, guide books, cash, house keys, car keys... to say nothing of mobiles and chargers. I think Giles's mother is rather dependent on us going out for part of the day so she can relax herself, rather than having us there twenty-four-seven – or nine-eleven, as Giles insists on describing it.

<u>Monday 15th</u>

GILES: All quiet back in Wiltshire but the courgettes have turned into marrows. I put them on a chair outside the field gate with a sign saying 'FREE ESSEX MARROWS'. This year they were snapped up almost immediately. A sign of the times and food shortages.

MARY: Why not free Wiltshire marrows? This is an example of Giles having Hatrolallia. His explanation, 'But I used to live in Essex and a man in the next village would always have a sign outside his house saying "FREE ESSEX MARROWS".'

GILES: I went to fill up at the local garage and found it surprisingly empty. It seems all our neighbours were indoors watching the Olympics. Why should I be made to feel guilty about not joining in? Even David Attenborough has said, 'There are a few people in the country who don't want necessarily to see people with very few clothes on jumping off something.'

MARY: I'm not sporty. I'm badly co-ordinated and the best I can hope for is a vigorous uphill walk. I never even thought of running on concrete since it does your knees in in later life, and I've been told by a personal trainer that a woman should never run, either on concrete or on a gym running machine. She should only walk uphill fast or use the uphill walking machine at the gym. Otherwise she risks developing the dread condition of 'banana bosom'. Why don't people make the connection between the pounding and the loss of elasticity?

I recently wrote an article about neck lifts during which I met the famous Harley Street surgeon Rajid Grover. He told me something reassuring, which is that, 'All women's necks go at the age of about forty-three and, unless the woman has done something silly like pavement pounding, it is just something physiological and nothing the woman herself can be blamed for.'

As for watching sport – I followed Wimbledon one year while helping to nurse my sick father and found very quickly that it was absolutely compelling once you got a taste for it. I can't remember who I was interested in – perhaps it was that black-haired tennis player Ilie Nastase. Anyway, I took each shot he won as a personal triumph and ditto when he was knocked out I was devastated. I had invested so much emotional energy in him winning.

I haven't watched sport since because, apart from not having time because of being so busy cleaning, I can't help but, in the words of Rudyard Kipling, treat those two impostors, triumph and disaster, just the same.

Sunday 28th

MARY: A breakthrough. As a result of our *Men are from Mars, Women are from Venus* style diary experiment, we have resolved a long-standing argument over the kitchen.

Our galley-style kitchen is revolting and everyone who has been here would agree. Above all we need a new sink. The one we have is stained. The tap heads have come off leaving traps for gunk that we have to look at every day. Yet Giles has been adamant that we cannot replace them.

GILES: It is a perfectly good sink. The mixer tap works very well and it has an ideological value for me because I remember the day when the plumber came to the cottage to replace the taps. I remember that it was the same day as either Bert or Polly's funeral and I remember leaving him to it as we went up to the church in our Sunday best and thinking – one good thing about Wiltshire is that you can trust a workman to be left alone in your cottage.

When we came back about an hour later, he gleefully announced that he had succeeded in stripping down the tap, descaling it and making it work again. He had spared us the cost of buying a new tap. Therefore, to me, when I look at this tap, even though the heads are still off it, it represents a triumph for the philosophy enshrined in the cult book of the Seventies *Zen and the Art of Motorcycle Maintenance* – in other words the opposite of built-in obsolescence. Instead of instant replacement and landfill clogging, he had restored the flow by the traditional virtues of patience and time.

The fact that the taps are still going years later, rather than having submitted to the excessively hard water which comes from the private reservoir our village draws from, gives me a sense of satisfaction each time I see them gush. We each make our own reality.

Yes, the open heads act as repositories for gunk and yes there is a spidery area where the wooden work surface has rotted away at the back of the sink (caveat emptor – don't buy wooden sink surrounds, they are a nightmare) but I'm not looking at them. I am looking out of the window at the fine trees I have planted outside and the sunbeams playing on the tall, waving Cosmos, whose daisy-like mauve and purple heads refuse to accept that winter is around the corner.

Re: the kitchen: it's a galley kitchen and it still works – just. I believe in keeping things that still work. The whole myth of the kitchen being the heart of the house and the biggest room where children do projects on a massive table has not materialised in the cottage. We are the only ones amongst our friends who lack an AGA. In this way we are imposters. Neither, incidentally, do we possess that other badge of Yuppie honour – a sit on mower.

Our kitchen is ten foot by six and a half and would not look amiss in a boat. Our friend Jo says that we eat far too many roasts. But then she adds she doesn't blame us because, 'your kitchen is so small you haven't got any chopping surfaces for salad or marinating fish.' Well-designed, it does suffer from the fact that we employed some school leavers to put on cheap B&Q plastic floor tiles and they were trying to do the project against the clock in order to get to a party in London on the same day as they laid them. One by one the tiles have been popping out ever since.

My parents also embraced the make-do-and-mend philosophy. My father believed that any money he 'got in' or 'fresh' money (they always got money in through selling houses and moving to smaller ones, rather than earning it) should not be used unnecessarily. They were always keen to save money and so they regretted having splashed out on a fashionable ceramic hob cooker using their tiny unearned income to buy it. They found they

GROTTAGE KITCHEN

resented the enormous amount of energy required to get up to a workable degree of red hot heat only to their dismay, to then have to observe the residual energy being dissipated into the ether as a waste product, half an hour after they had turned off the hob. 'Bugger the ceramic hob, ' said my father who resurrected a camping gas pair of rings from the garage, attached to a Primus Stove which they placed over the ceramic hob, only using the hob for major religious festivals like Easter and Christmas. Besides my parents had signed up for an electricity programme called Economy 7 which allowed them to pay less per unit if they were to use the bulk of their electricity in, for example, the middle of the night. This meant that having to use the oven to cook dinner any time other than between two and four in the morning, they would pay a punitive rate. And so they naturally used the camping gas stove.

MARY: Reading the above means that, after years of bitterness about the kitchen – pop-up bitterness that is, not permanent – I suddenly see why Giles wants to leave the taps as they are. I now see that his aspirations are just different from those of the average Briton who wants a display kitchen. It's not sadism after all, but an admirable aspiration to make do and mend. This is the sort of thing that comes under the heading 'men are from Mars and women are from Venus'. Regarding the kitchen, in any case Giles does almost all the cooking – not because he's a new man or because I can't cook but I just haven't time for any leisurely activities where I can't multi-task. While I slave away at the ironing board (I can multi task by listening to instructive radio) or single-mindedly at the computer, Giles is happily whiling away the hours as he perfectionises sauces, decides he needs some wild garlic for a lamb joint and makes a forty-minute round trip to the wood above the house to get some... Also, he is very good at it.

GILES: The reason I like to cook is that way I can get the food the way I like it. I feel I may suffer from a condition called Culinary Hypersensitivity Disorder (CHD). In short, my taste buds may be over-sensitive. Although Mary once made a successful brown bread ice cream, all too often I find fault with her efforts, especially if she has cooked meat. She seems to aspire to the 'Land of Leather' cooking method where all meat must be incinerated.

However, the real reason I rule the kitchen is more to do with division of labour and attention to detail. Mary doesn't have the time to ensure everything can be simultaneously *au point*... I do and I can go into the lane verges and pick chives and Jack-by-the-hedge which lends a piquant mustard flavour to salads or up to the wood to forage for wild garlic leaves for *omelettes aux fines herbes* for example. Even though I think the foraging craze has now become worthy of satire.

I always have time to prepare things. Mary doesn't because she is in a rush. Hence sub-optimal fayre is served. Since I bought a Lidl non-stick ceramic pan and my mother explained that you do not have to get it as hot as previously, omelettes and crêpes, Rosie's favourite, have been the way forward.

MARY: I have enjoyed cooking on the few occasions I've had time to but Giles tends to keep coming into the tiny kitchen to criticise me which is, of course, undermining. I read an article by Sarah Vine the other day in which she revealed that she becomes a monster when Michael Gove enters their kitchen. She immediately begins carping and telling him, for example, not to put tomatoes into the fridge when he had no intention of so doing. She ends by admitting that if he ever finds out he is perfectly capable of doing all the cooking himself, Sarah Vine will feel less secure about his need for her. There's a whiff of the same thing with Giles and his competitiveness over the kitchen but in a way this suits me because I really do work twenty-four-seven and have no time for the leisurely pursuit of real cooking.

Giles also boasts that he is in charge of washing up. Yes, but I have begun to notice Parkinson's Law kicking in. In Parkinson's Law, an activity expands to fit the amount of time available for it. Giles has begun to take rather too long about loading the dishwasher every morning (he's 'too tired' to do it before bed).

And so, as I am boiling an egg or the kettle (both for five minutes) I enjoy the challenge of seeing if I can unload and reload the dishwasher before the five minutes are up. Usually I can. Whereas Giles seems to take up to twenty minutes to do it each morning.

GILES: The dishwasher is my territory and I don't appreciate Mary's cheating me of that satisfying work each morning which helps me to 'come round' as I'm waiting for the caffeine to kick in, and gain a foot-hold onto the day, to use an analogy with mountain climbing. I also need to control the loading of the dish-washer. Mary is inclined to put in food-caked plates and, following an incident yesterday I've banned her from loading the dishwasher at all as I noticed an electronic warning signal asking for both water and rinse aid. On inspection, I found the drainage basket loaded to the hilt with guinea fowl bones and roast potatoes which Mary had flung carelessly in in her bid to compete against me with the loading time.

MARY: Giles called me down from my desk in Room Two for a ticking-off like I was some kind of schoolgirl during the Idi Amin regime in Uganda. At first I was genuinely ashamed of having thrown in so many bones but, looking more closely at Idi's 'evidence' of my incompetence, I smelt a rat. There were simply a few too many bones – I mean a leg and a wing. There's no way I wouldn't have scraped them off the plates for boiling up as stock. In short

Giles had clearly stooped so low as to 'plant' the evidence against me.

GILES: We've been too busy all these years to call in psychic house cleaners or Feng Shui experts but there is no doubt about it – there are bad vibes in the kitchen and Mary and I have most of our arguments in there.

Having been brought up with sub-optimal kitchen equipment, I think this kitchen of ours in Wiltshire is normal. I prefer hand-mincers for example over Magimixes and I create breadcrumbs by placing the oven dried slices of Mother's Pride in a paper envelope inside a plastic bag and then standing on it till the desired consistency is achieved. Our few guests have commented that these home made and home seasoned breadcrumbs trump all shop-bought varieties. I use them on my trademark fishcakes.

I like secondary or intermediate technology and don't want to join the technological race or introduce unnecessary innovations such as have been installed by friends who have given up kettles and instead have taps which gush scalding water on demand. We don't even have a microwave. This is partly in the perhaps half-baked belief that this will help us to dodge cancer, but also because there is no room for one in the tiny kitchen.

My other objection is that all the carpenters in this area are in such high demand we could never get one to commit to us.

MARY: But why can't Giles tackle the job himself? Cyril says it's because 'Giles hates progress'.

GILES: Cyril's quite right. I don't like things moving forward. I would describe myself as a 'yes but' man.

My strength is in complaining. If the status quo gets better, I have less to complain about. It's like a mental block... I become attached to the mental block. If the farmers around here suddenly turned organic, I would lose my *raison d'être*. Correction: my reason for hand-wringing.

I found I could identify with those members of the so-called deaf who formed a pressure group to unite against a simple operation which could have cured their condition. They objected because they would thereby lose their special status which was a badge of identity that they clung to.

It was the philosopher Gurdjieff who noted that many men are attached to their suffering. If you take it away from them they will have an identity crisis. I believe this is the basis for the popularity of Corbyn – he allows the sullen and defeated hordes to unite in resentment. Being a victim is so much easier than embracing the philosophy of self-reliance.

MARY: I'll be uniting with them in resentment too.

SEPTEMBER

Thursday 1st

GILES: Mary has been to Lacock Garden Centre to look at garden sheds. She employed a jobless graduate neighbour of 22 to drive her there since she can't drive herself. I have refused to look at sheds unless she will agree that what we need in the one acre field is a starter home for our older daughter and not a shed in which to store Mary's clutter from Northern Ireland – Victorian sideboards, burst horsehair chaises longues, Victorian bed pans, and grotesque Hyacinth Bucket-style Sheffield plate hors d'oeuvres platters and the like.

MARY: It's all very well Giles saying we need to build a starter home for our daughter but the contract we signed when we bought the cottage specifically disallowed us from building any residential dwellings in the one acre field. Giles thinks we can get around this because his late father, who is his role model, succeeded in doing precisely this in his own back yard. He built, from scratch, 'stables' in an area of outstanding natural beauty in Cheshire. Then had the planning officer round for drinks – it was the 1970s. Was it Hirondelle or Lutomer Riesling that he offered?

GILES: This was the first time in history that wine was democratised and freely available to the common man, and not just the ones who could order crates from Tanners, the wine merchants in Shrewsbury. Either way, Godfrey managed to get the official 'squiffy' enough to sign off a 'change of use' from equine to residential.

MARY: Giles's main focus in life has always been to tread exactly the same path trodden by his father. Which is worrying since his father died at 65.

GILES: We have an issue with power in this marriage. Mary may earn more money than I do but, according to my Jungian analyst, Mr Newman, this does not give her the divine right to rule. He who pays the piper calls the tune, says Mary. Yet even now I have power over Mary because I won't write to a friend who had us to stay for the weekend because her eighteen-year-old son spilt milk in the back of the Volvo which probably means we'll have to sell the car as you can never get rid of the smell of spilt milk.

In praise of cow parsley

Friday 2nd

MARY: I only wish I did have some power over Giles. I have none at all. He won't go to parties in London to which I often suspect I've only been invited because people really want him to come, and not particularly me. And he bitterly resists my suggesting we have people to dinner, always saying 'let's leave it till the weather is better'. I can't stop him having eco-wars with the two billionaire neighbours with whom we 'march'. He's constantly rushing out to complain about the sprays and the over-zealous strimming that takes place around us.

One good thing, though, is that this May there was no spraying of the cow parsley in the verges. This is thanks to Giles. Giles believes in leaving things untidy to provide habitat for overwintering invertebrates, while he accuses our neighbours of favouring the 'squaddie haircut' school of neatness (i.e., beautifully mown lawns and tidy verges) which means, says Giles, 'death to biodiversity'. And 'tidy mindedness is the enemy of conservation'.

Having been brought up in Northern Ireland during the Troubles, the last thing I want is to make enemies of our neighbours, but I have no power over him at all *vis-à-vis* conciliation and suggesting we have the spraying neighbours round for dinner.

I bear in mind that his childhood was characterised by 'neighbour wars' between his role model father and all three of the neighbours around them in their converted stables in Cheshire. One of the problems arose because a neighbour stabled his horses on Godfrey's land at a peppercorn rent and then claimed an agricultural tenancy.

Giles has therefore 'inherited' an irrational suspicion that his neighbours, like Godfrey's neighbours, are trying to somehow get one over on the gullible 'yuppie incomer'.

The word yuppie of course, has not been used by anyone other than Giles since the 1980s but he was struck, on our arrival in the village in 1988, by overhearing our then next-door neighbour Polly, the wife of Bert, talking about how the village (of thirteen houses – nearly all of which, apart from the Manor Farm and the Old Rectory, had traditionally been occupied by members of her own family, the Vardens) had changed. 'It's all yuppies now,' she grumbled. And as Giles likes to cling to negative things I often hear him describing himself, thirty years on, as a 'yuppie', with its implied disapproval. This despite him not fitting into any of the identifiers of the original moniker which was used to describe upwardly mobile young professionals.

The only time I can get him to stop doing something I really mind about is when I head for the village post-box with a twenty-pound note in one hand and a stamped addressed envelope to our neighbour Ben Goodall in the other. As I insert the note into the envelope to despatch the anonymous present, Giles will normally back down. He can't bear to think of Goodall getting free money through the post.

Ben Goodall is a rival painter in the Vale of Pewsey, tackling very much the same sort of subjects pictorially as does Giles, for the same clients. In the past Ben tackled portraits; now, like Giles, he tackles interiors. The Easel Wars have been raging for twenty years or more.

GILES: The problem is that because Ben Goodall does so much work – apparently he posts a new painting or drawing on the internet almost every day – he is becoming better and better and is now almost as good as me.

MARY: He might as well be since Giles seems no longer to be a working artist.

Friday 16th

MARY: We are driving up to Norfolk to stay with Desmond, who exemplifies our shared taste for bossy and eccentric friends. On the way, we slowed to pass a peculiar shrine where someone had committed suicide off a bridge. Tragic of course – but why do mourners leave the cellophane on? It reminded us of the time we went to Kensington Palace after the death of Princess Diana. Giles and I were swept up in the mood of national mourning and mass hysteria at the time but even so we couldn't help wondering why people didn't take the flowers out of the cello-phane and what they thought was going to happen to the sodden soft toys after a week in the rain.

One of the last legacies of the Peace Agreement, i.e., when we went to counselling in the local surgery it was agreed that if I stopped rushing out of the house to yell at Giles to stop mowing, he would stop driving at 50 mph on the dangerously curvy A345.

To reward him for driving reasonably safely to Norwich, I've downloaded some podcasts on subjects of interest to Giles and though not to me; perhaps we can bond if I try to be interested by listening to it together with him.

One example was a radio item about 'whooping', in which Howard Jacobson decried the new trend for audiences to whoop in public scenarios, thus effec-tively gagging the performer on the stage. Another was an interview with Piers Corbyn, brother of Jeremy, on LBC. Who would have believed that Corbyn 2, a meteorologist who makes his living by using sunspots to successfully predict long-term weather patterns, would be on the side of Donald Trump re: climate change, but there he was saying that Trump had seen through the 'myth' of the greenhouse effect. 'There is no evidence at all that climate change is manmade,' said Corbyn, who does not deny climate change, he just says there is no evidence to support the claim that manmade CO_2 is the cause of it.

GILES: Shared disapproval is still a bonding factor for Mary and me. We also share horror in the same words. Neither of us likes the word Hainault, plaudit, or leccy. Often when we are driving on a long journey together we see, from the relative security of the Volvo window, plenty to disapprove of – particularly the bunches of flowers in cellophane at accident blackspots.

We hate the emotional incontinence of the new Cry Baby Britain where the camera seems to linger in expectation that anybody who is vulnerable (dread word) who doesn't well up and blub in front of the camera, is almost in breach of contract.

We dislike hugging, fridge-magnet clichés and the absurd over-reaction of contestants in television elimination contests who never act like the good losers of old who embraced, as in our day, 'It's not the winning but it's the taking part' philosophy but act as though their lives, following elimination, are effectively over, since being on this show was their last chance of fame and therefore happiness. The rot started with John Major who introduced the something-for-nothing culture of the lottery.

MARY: Giles dislikes the new 'liberated' television adverts for sanitary towels and pile cream and incontinence pads. Taboos are broken daily. He dislikes the new unpleasant trend of showing people, in television plays, sitting on the loo, even 'shaking' the drips'. 'It's only a matter of time until the cameras are positioned actually in the lavatory bowl itself to make the programme more gritty.'

Neither of us like to see septua- and octogenarians being encouraged by the likes of Esther Rantzen to behave in undignified manner, being crude or pandering to dumb Britain. We are mystified by cuddly toys at funerals or by people singing 'I did it my way'.

GILES: So much of reality television is a thinly disguised freak show. Freak shows were popular in this country from around the mid-sixteenth century to 1884 when Joseph Merrick, the Elephant Man, was at the peak of his fame, but since they are now effectively banned we have to watch dishonest documentaries posturing as cutting edge celebrations of diversity instead. 'Thirty Stone Child', 'The Woman Who Ate Her Own House', 'Half Man Half Tree'. This unwholesome trend in broadcasting makes us all too often feel like strangers in a strange land.

Saturday 24th

MARY: If I could be spared one recurring event in my life it would be the quarterly requirement for me to prepare the papers for the accountant. It's a lonely and thankless and fiddly task, handling thermo-printed receipts which have mainly faded and seeking bank and credit card statements some of which, although I have fastidiously stored them in a pile as they came in, have mysteriously gone missing.

Today I begged Giles to help me with this two-day chore.

'What does it involve?' he asked restlessly.

'It involves one person reading things out, the other one ticking boxes and sliding slimy fading receipts on thermal paper into plastic envelopes.'

'I'd like to help you,' replied Giles (I know this because I recorded it on voice memos), 'but I won't be able to because I've been away for seven days.'

'Why is that logical?' I asked.

'Well, a lot has gone on in the garden since I've been away.'

'Yet you agree that the accountancy chore has to be done so who do you think should do it – given that it's to your own benefit?'

'Mine takes much less time to do than yours because I don't spend anything.'

This is the sort of impasse I don't enjoy arriving at during one of the most tortuous points of the quarter. But my guru Betty Parsons taught me to turn setbacks to my advantage and, considering the possible benefits of Giles *not* helping with the paperwork I realised it WOULD be to my advantage if he didn't get a chance to study the receipts for my spendings. So I suggested that, if he wasn't prepared to help with the accountancy work, 'maybe you would help me instead by writing thank you letters to Cyril, Desmond and Melissa?'

Giles replied, 'Not to Melissa, not for yet another inedible lunch. But I will write to Cyril and Desmond. Very short letters but not to Melissa. '

This sort of illogicality makes me wonder whether, not jokingly, Giles doesn't have just Variable Intelligence Disorder but perhaps early onset dementia.

I calmly reminded him that the rules of society are that the person who has made the effort to create a lovely scenario in which Giles could bond again with an old friend he hadn't seen for a bit, have lunch, and bring his daughter to lunch, needs to be thanked.

'And for you not to thank her, on the grounds that the meal was inedible, suggests you have sustained some kind of brain damage – perhaps from inhaling agricultural sprays?'

Giles has been thrilled that this morning's paper carried a report that pesticides do damage brains.

'Well all right. I'll use the last three postcards of the Nikolai Astrup. But you must tell Christof [our neighbour on the hill above us] that we'll only go to the Outside Chance with him on the strict understanding that we will be back here by 10 pm.'

'To watch telly?'

'No. Not just telly! Desmond on telly! At ten o'clock!'

'Giles, may I ask you something? Do you think you would enjoy living with you, if you were me?'

'No, I wouldn't. But I've just realised what's wrong with me. I'm starving. No wonder I'm bad tempered. Where are the Medjool dates, Mary?'

'And don't tell me you had more than one cup of coffee this morning?'

'I'm afraid I had three. I needed three to wake me up. Didn't you hear that hornet in the night making intermittent rasping noises?'

OCTOBER

Monday 3rd

GILES: The *Daily Mail* has finally run a piece about the oestrogenisation of the water supply. It's something I've been banging on about for seventeen years, when my eco-chum Mike drew it to my attention that the polar bears in Antarctica had begun to show intersex features and deformed genitalia. Even as far away as Antarctica the oestrogen (an exquisitely potent hormone which resists filtering during water recycling) from the 'developed' world was making its mark. But as I said to Mike, 'You don't have to go to the Antarctic. Think of every married couple we know. The man is slaving away in the kitchen while the woman is holding forth at the top of the table.'

MARY: I agree with most of Giles's eco-ranting. I'm just too busy to rant myself. And it's clear that all the contraceptive pills and hormone replacement therapy going into our water supply are taking their toll. It's good that 2016 man is in touch with his feelings and can cry and be metrosexual but name me a butch man in British public life today who exudes the same levels of testosterone as did Sir Winston Churchill, Errol Flynn or Sir Patrick Leigh Fermor – Mick Jagger? David Beckham? Boris is the exception that proves the rule.

I'm not saying I don't welcome the feminisation of men. It's just as well it's happening simultaneously to the masculinisation of women. Remember the days when women fainted and screamed and stood on chairs if they saw mice? In films they were always clutching jewel boxes and being hysterical when fires broke out. They cowered during dramas and let the men take charge.

But could women have ever actually been so weedy in real life? Well, only fifty years ago Audrey Hepburn's vital statistics were 34-20-34 and she had a tinkling melodious voice, while my own body is a continuous column 40-40-40 and my voice can turn really corncrake under stress. I have read that constant rushes of adrenaline, as a woman tries to compete in a man's world, send spurts of testosterone into her body. Also, because men lack imagination, the woman has many more rushes of cortisol, the fear hormone, which is closely allied to testosterone.

Thursday 6th

GILES: The whole village seems to be enthralled by the Keanu Reeves-lookalike Dave Dewey the thatcher, who is currently tackling our end of the cottage thatch. The traffic has even increased as women seem to be taking the long way round after they've dropped their children at the local school so they can ogle him.

Mary had to forcibly stop me from putting out three large 'NO LOITERING' signs I had prepared and was about to position on the roadside complete with circular arrows to suggest traffic, both human and vehicular, should keep moving. Mary said that the whole point of living in a village is that we are supposed to celebrate the slow quality of life versus the dog-eat-dog rat-race of the city.

The previous thatcher, Royston Stagg, was a smoker and a superb thatcher who worked thoroughly at the pace of vegetative growth. He could be said to have invented slow thatching and took frequent cigarette breaks in his station wagon parked in our field gate, dreamily puffing and gazing contentedly at the vista of downland in the distance. This suited us well; it gave us time to earn the money to pay him. We gave him frequent cups of tea as well to add more leisure time. Oddly our neighbour Polly got in the act as well.

Polly next door in the terrace never conferred with us regarding the timing of our own tea-making ceremonies so even more delay ensued as poor Royston, who had just scaled a thirty foot ladder, with all the effort of John Noakes scaling Nelson's Column, would be hailed by Polly for another cuppa. 'Roy-stern? Roy-stern? Roy-stern? Where are you lurve?' she would quail through the beech hedge. 'Cuppa tea lurve?'

With infinite patience and kindness the breathless thatcher would reply, 'Down in a mo, Polly.'

MARY: To this day Giles frequently shouts to himself 'Roy-stern? Roy-stern? Roy-stern?' for no particular reason, but often while washing up or sweeping the floor, and even though dear Polly is now pushing up daisies in our village graveyard and Stewart, whose family have been thatching in a continuous line for three hundred years, has shut up shop and retired.

GILES: As to the quality of thatching straw? Reed, which is traditionally used in Devon and Norfolk, would seem a better choice since it grows in an aquatic environment, but it's all long straw, derived from wheat crops, in this arable district. It was a cheap and available roofing material in the days when labour was cheap and carter's lads were whipped cruelly by their masters. But, just as bread is today nutritionally deficient compared to the 'staff of life' it represented in our grandpa's day, so I believe that straw is not what it once was. The tendency to give the wheat a boost with artificial nitrogen makes the straw more sappy, more watery and have less dry matter compared to organic straw. But then, organic straw would send the roofing bill soaring by an extra £10,000.

'Country life? That's going to cost you,' according to Martin Ellis, a housing economist at the Halifax writing in *The Times* today. 'The countryside continues to attract homeowners inspired by open spaces, a cleaner environment and the prospect of a potentially greater quality of life.'

However, the reality is that Fleur, our eldest daughter seems to have become allergic to thatch and sneezes uncontrollably if she is in the cottage for more than thirty-six hours. As is my elderly volcanologist friend and neighbour who lives on the other side of the Downs. Roswitha can only partake of tea and cake *outside* the cottage and while sitting in our spinney. I am disillusioned with thatch. Warm duvet in winter it ain't; cool duvet in summer it ain't, but it can be guaranteed to attract every sort of fauna into the home, including wrens, bats, squirrels, shrews, mice or worse as they come in their hordes seeking a refuge from the inhospitable prairies outside.

Dave Dewey is a great thatcher and craftsman who straddles the class divide between the Wiltshire indigenous folk and the incomers or 'yuppies', as the natives refer to us. He is a social chameleon who has mastered both dialects and slides effortlessly into whichever one befits his interlocutor. His film star looks are still stopping traffic. Tall, dark, lean and angular, he doesn't carry a shred of extra poundage on account of spending his days shinning up ladders with sheaves of thatching straw. He carries antiquated tools such as billhooks for fashioning hazel spars and ledgers to bind the thatch. Thatching is a traditional craft where there are no short cuts, which is why thatchers are usually trim.

Gardeners, on the other hand, have quad bikes and, freed from the tyranny of sweeping leaves by using petrol blowers, are becoming increasingly rotund in appearance as are many of the traditional labouring classes. We see evidence of this every year at the annual Steam Fair at nearby Rainscombe, where antique tractors, train engines and animal traps are on display. Each year, an increasing preponderance of BMIs in the Overweight or Obese categories signal how toilers in the field have been replaced by the modern machine.

As brawn and sinew are replaced by subcutaneous lard, it's no wonder that the Wiltshire people are sometimes nicknamed 'lardy cakes' after the famous animal-fat rich pastry available from our local bakery, which, once tasted, becomes addictive.

Not me, of course. I do everything by hand.

Wednesday 19th

MARY: Dave Dewey was banging and moving on the scaffolding all around the window of Room Two from about eight in the morning, even though I had the curtains down and could easily have still been asleep. We had Louise and Gretel (wife of Ben Goodall) over to lunch. Louise is a benevolent local landowner who, for some reason, enjoys coming to our cottage and washing up.

Gretel and I are the best of friends despite our husbands being engaged in the Easel Wars. Like the Schleswig-Holstein Question, the Easel Wars are a complex set of diplomatic and other issues whose origins are lost in the midst of time.

Giles always tries to find out what is the latest smart commission Ben is currently undertaking. So he joined us for lunch. Giles lit a log fire for us and cooked first-rate fishcakes using smoked haddock and coley, before going into the garden to allow us to thrash through some issues. When I mentioned that our thatcher was very glamorous Louise said, 'Oh. I wonder if he's the one who's going out with Virginia Smail. I know she has a new boyfriend who's a thatcher. I wonder if it's him.'

I went outside on the pretext of talking to Dave about the weather and if he thought it would hold long enough to allow him to complete the job. He was standing by his truck fiddling with some string and he asked if my guest was OK with where she was parked as she seemed to be a little bit uncertain where to put her BMW. 'Well it's surprising if she was uncertain,' I said. 'That's Louise Brewer. She's been coming here for thirty years. You may know her if you follow the hunt.'

'Well,' volunteered Dave Dewey. 'I should do. Or I will soon in any case. My new girlfriend is chairman of the hunt.'

'Really?' I feigned surprise.

'Yeah – well we come from very different worlds as you can imagine. But I've met her parents and it went OK. Nice bloke, Her dad.'

Louise was fascinated when I went inside. Giles suddenly appeared in the room to advance his theory that cases of migration between classes are rare in Wiltshire where, according to Giles, 'we seem to *want* a class-ridden society unlike most Britons who say they don't. This is because this area still has Big Houses and still needs people to work in them. Deference, therefore, where deference is due, i.e., not to 'Rock Squires' and the like, still hangs on in the satellites to the Big House.'

'That's absolute rubbish, Giles,' said Louise Brewer, 'and all in your own mind.'

And to do with him being stuck in the Seventies.

NOVEMBER

Tuesday 8th

MARY: As I was applying moisturiser this morning in the upstairs bathroom off the miniature library, Giles suddenly burst into the cottage (from the garden as usual) and I heard his voice shouting 'Mary! Mary! Mary!'

Eventually I had to come to the top of the stairs. 'Quickly,' said Giles. 'Quickly, get a cushion we don't want. Quickly! I'm a busy man. I've no time for explanations.'

It turned out that he'd seen a sixty-something workman, completely bald-headed (in the manner of Yul Brynner in *The King and I*) kneeling on Sandi Harrison's doorstep, doing some sort of grouting and, since he had no kneeling mat, Giles, who had been spying on him from the scaffolding, realised he must have been in agony. I said we didn't have any cushions we didn't want; however I put one inside a plastic bag to protect it and brought it along to the boiler-suited workman, who had a weather-beaten face.

Since Giles doesn't like to use up 'emotional energy' talking to people, he got me to do it for him. The man, called Patrick, told me he is a specialist in brickwork and woodwork and that he used to work on stately homes and historic buildings but now he wants to work around here as he lives locally and would be able to cycle to work. When he brought the cushion back later, we chatted to him and we felt that he seems to be on Giles's wavelength eco-wise.

Wednesday 9th

MARY: We have been so missing Gug and his fellow bed blockers. It's one of the most stressy things about living in a cottage with twelve rooms because Giles likes to call me from the room he is standing in, and then start saying in that room whatever it is he has to say.

I then have to scuttle downstairs or otherwise towards him, invariably arriving at the tail end of his speech only to have him berate me saying, 'I'm a busy man. The master of the house doesn't expect to have to repeat himself.'

It doesn't occur to him that he should come to look for me first, and then start speaking.

But none of it matters if we have a live-in Gug because then I get the 'sympathy vote' and often the Gugs question their master. 'Giles,' they ask, 'why don't you go into the room where you know Mary to be sitting rather than calling her from a few rooms away?'

One of the reasons I found Gug One's presence in the cottage so agreeable was that he used to run on his young legs to whichever room Giles was calling from and then run back on them to the room I was in to report, like Mercury, whatever it was that Giles wanted and then back again with my response. This all added to the sense of calm that would prevail when Gug was resident. We envy our richer contemporaries Buster and Sharon who have an intercom system in their large cottage, which means that every so often a disembodied voice enters every room saying something like 'have you seen my black trainers?' and then the other person calmly replies yes or no. No shouting need take place.

Cyril offered to buy me, not Giles, a loudhailer as used by coxes in the sport of competitive rowing so that I don't have to yell my lungs out to get Giles in from the garden, but I think this would introduce too brutal an element into the country atmosphere. However, we both agree Giles has more time on his hands than I do so if he wants me, he doesn't need a loudhailer he can just come in from the garden and wander at his leisure around all the twelve rooms till he finds me.

So, because tension in the cottage has been unnecessarily high in the absence of Gugs, I've taken steps and tonight we've got a new starter Gug coming to stay before starting work for me tomorrow morning. He's a good-natured and intelligent chap, and at 22, young enough to still think it quite fun to work for me and Giles... I've told him that the other Gugs have all gone on to be extremely successful.

Friday 11th

MARY: Gug Six was on my side when Giles came back from the hairdresser, Ingrid, at Curl Up & Dye. As he left for the salon after breakfast, Giles announced to Gug Six that he was going to ask for what he called a 'knuckle cut', as by having it cut extra short this would mean he could get the value of two haircuts for the price of one.

'But that would be self-sabotage Giles!' marvelled Gug Six. 'Surely you wouldn't want to look terrible?'

When Giles returned he'd clearly thought better of asking for a knuckle cut. He still looked much worse though. And although he has a very thick head of hair and is absolutely not balding anywhere on his head, Ingrid has, for reasons best known to herself, created a weird new parting on the back of his head which makes him look as though the thick thatch at the front was a comb-over as in Robert Robinson's day.

Gug Six took a picture of the back of Giles's head with his mobile and showed it to Giles to show him what we meant.

I expected him to be dismayed. Instead dimples appeared in his cheeks (a sign that he's happy). 'That's absolutely hideous,' he enthused. 'What on earth inspired Ingrid to do that?'

'Did you ask her to?'

'Well, yes,' he confessed, 'and Ingrid takes the view that the customer is always right. She's always done me proud.'

Sunday 13th

MARY: When I was pregnant with our first baby, we didn't ask the sonographer to tell us what sex it was – we wanted it to be a surprise. Just as we used to enjoy getting films developed in the chemist for the very same reason. But many of the layman observers told us we were expecting a boy. So we were prepared for one, although they were wrong. I was amazed when Giles insisted that the baby must be called Charles. Why? It seemed so poncey as a name and with no relevance to anyone in our family. Then I overheard him chuckling on the telephone to his brother Pip.

'I'm going for the name Charles. It means, later on, when Mary is calling one of us we can pretend we thought she was calling for the other one. Really good potential for wind-ups.'

Unfortunately, Giles seems to thrive on tension, both low and high grade. It's one of the reasons why he encourages Phoebe, our Tibetan Spaniel, to stand at the window of Room Two, or indeed at any window to which he could climb onto the sill of, to bark.

GILES: My feeling is that a Tibetan Spaniel should be allowed to fulfil the role of his ancestors, which

KNUCKLE CUT

is to take up a viewing point high on the monastery wall and with his exceptional eyesight be able to spot and announce the arrival of strangers heading from a great distance across the plains towards the monastery so the monks could send out the mastiffs in defence.

By enabling the dog to yap as much as he liked, it would make him feel happy that he was protecting his family, since, apart from keeping monks' thighs warm, this is what the dog was bred for.

But I was ticked off the other day by Stewart Vardens because our dog's barking meant that he couldn't hear the music. 'What music?' I asked. 'The music of the hounds', he replied. This seemed a rather elevated thought from someone I had thought of as a gardener and terrier man. It had never occurred to me Stewart could regard the barking of the hounds with such poetic feeling as to describe it as music, and it means that I now shut Phoebe up when the hounds are in the area.

MARY: Room Four is where Phoebe jumps onto the sofa to have his harness fitted and then his lead clipped onto it. Scenting my walking boots, he came eagerly towards me. Phoebe's made us very happy. Owning a dog, in my view, is only partly about the affection and the guaranteed welcome when you come through the door. In a world where humans are complicated and difficult to please, at least you can be sure of making one domestic being blissfully happy – your dog. A dog just wants walks, company and regular food to guarantee his happiness.

So today I took him out for a four thousand step walk, measured on the health app of my iPhone, and he came jauntily behind me with tail high, walking all the way off the lead. Now that he is older he no longer has the appetite for chasing sheep that he had when young. Nothing could give him a greater sense of power than being able to round up a whole flock of much bigger animals and end up with one of them, lying on her back, bicycling as Phoebe went in for the jugular. We had two very near misses *vis-à-vis* Phoebe being shot by the farmer. Farmers have no compunction in shooting a badly-behaved dog because sheep-worrying is a very real problem.

When I got back to the cottage our neighbour Jake the sweep was standing outside talking to Dave Dewey, the thatcher. Jake is rather magnificent, a sort of column of countryman with all the characteristics of John Bull, classically stout and stubborn. Jake bows to no one with any sort of conformity, he just dresses and acts to suit himself, with a thick beard and glistening eyes. Neither does he doff his cap to the residents of the 'Big House', despite living in this village for all of his seventy years. Giles likes to fantasise that Jake is descended from agricultural Luddites who, according to the Victorian nature writer Richard Jefferies, used to wreck machinery in this very area. In his mind,

Giles – an obsessive Richard Jefferies reader – likes to trace a direct line between now and then.

For twelve of those years Phoebe barked at the window every time Jake walked past with Ernie, his Lakeland terrier, as he led Ernie through the village and up past the church to the Downs. Even when Ernie died, Phoebe continued the maddening tradition of barking at the window, just at the sight of Jake.

'Don't stop him!' Giles always cooes. 'I like the sound of him barking.'

'You like it! You must be mad. What is there to like about barking?'

'It shows he still has spirit.'

Monday 14th

GILES: Mr Dewey has just popped a bill through the letter box for replacing the roof ridge and a large patch on the north side of the cottage.

MARY: I took Phoebe out for his walk. When I came back towards the cottage, I saw Dave Dewey next to his truck, tidying some bundles and rolling up some chicken netting. It was raining, so I didn't linger. I just said pleasantly, 'Oh thank you for your bill, Dave. I assume you don't want to be paid immediately.' After all, he only started five weeks ago.

'Well,' he countered. 'Not immediately. You could pay half immediately and then the rest of it at the end of next week when I've finished.'

GILES: This gave me a shock – who has got thousands of pounds in their current account apart from Sir Philip Green?

Mary says that must mean Dave is making a very handsome sum of money every week since he only started five weeks ago. Nice work if you can get it. But then he works nine-eleven.

A lot of the time because the job is on the street side with scaffolding he has been distracted by Jake the sweep and Stu the gardener, both of them Vardens, fox-hunting terrier men, descended from original beaker folk, so called because of their characteristic pottery vessels which can be seen in Devizes museum, and all unaware that they are chatting amiably in MY time. I am becoming vexed by this, and spend a lot of time twitching at the net curtains so to speak.

Even though I am physically standing a mere two yards from these village gossips to eavesdrop, on the other side of a one brick thick wall of a labourer's cottage – my own – I can't decipher a word that is being said on account of the patois in which all three men are speaking.

I'm convinced this patois is being deployed to confuse us 'yups'. There are gales of laughter to be shared and it's a lot more interesting than James O'Brien, the sanctimonious liberal pontificator on LBC which Mary substitutes for local birdsong. One in ten words I can hear and a lot of 'Oh well, better get on then', repeated over and over, before starting another conversation.

The one thing I would never dream of asking Dave Dewey is 'are you winning?' This is the maddening phrase repeated up and down the land by the well-meaning but patronising middle classes to any one who is labouring.

MARY: Giles's chippiness, we have agreed, is not based on reality but more to do with nostalgia for his boyhood when definite class divisions existed and his parents were constantly changing their accents depending on to whom they were speaking. He thinks it is a red herring as his general feeling of being persecuted by the village has been deconstructed by my going through each cottage one by one and getting him to admit that everyone in the village probably does like us, even despite his eco warrior stuff. I must admit, however, that Jake Vardens probably doesn't.

GILES: With hindsight, we should never have chosen to live under thatch – it drips on our clothes. Unlike in a normal house with guttering and drainpipes, it goes down the back of our necks. This is why we are gagging for a porch, with a place to put wellies and a bench to lever them off again. The constant drip drip drip can be Chinese water torture but then Mary says I'm mad anyway. As Richard Jefferies put it in *The Toilers in the Field*:

The cold wind comes through the ill-fitting sash and drives with terrible force under the door. Very often the floor is one step lower than the ground outside, and consequently there is a constant tendency in rainy weather for the water to run or soak in. The elm tree overhead, that appeared so picturesque in summer, is now a curse, for the great drops fall perpetually from it upon the thatch and on the pathway in front of the door. In great storms of wind it sways to and fro, causing no little alarm, and boughs are sometimes blown off it, and fall upon the roof.

The thatch of the cottage is saturated; the plants and grasses that almost always grow on it, and the moss, are vividly, rankly green; till all dripping, soaked, overgrown with weeds, the wretched place looks not unlike a dunghill.

Tuesday 15th

MARY: Looking back, Giles has reflected today, 'I would say that I have probably wasted a good ten years of my life in trying to prove that other people were bad and I was good in various lone wolf eco campaigns against palm oil production, cow parsley spraying and the methodology of planting new trees where there were already trees. Questioning the public funding for the ruination of an existing wild hedge which seemed to me wasteful and unecolog-ical, grubbing up these older trees which could have been coppiced or pollarded in order to put in the same bog-standard euro mix of mixed hedges of the same varieties no doubt grown from saplings in Holland up and down the country making no concession to regional variations.'

His eco activities make him occasionally para-noid when we are driving in the nearby lanes.

The locals are always friendly towards me but it is a difficult juggling act since whenever we are driving and another vehicle approaches Giles always hisses, 'Don't wave! Just lift one finger of acknowledgement. Or do a knowing head swivel.' But as the passenger I can't do this since I'm not gripping a steering wheel. And I can't depend on Giles to do it since he rather relishes conflict. Moreover, he often spurts when he sees someone we know coming towards us because this will trigger a rictus of fear and anxiety in my face and preclude my beaming pleasantly as I scream 'Stop it Giles!'

I am not one of those people who memorises number plates and nor can I differentiate between types of cars, unless they are Minis or Volkswagen Beetles. Hence I consider it sensible to just wave vaguely at everyone we pass... just in case I know them.

GILES: Live and let live ought to be the watchword by which villagers rub along together, cheek by jowl, in the case of our own terraced row. Our next-door neighbours are delightful, the best we have ever had since the legendary old timers Bert and Polly. The new people, Mick and Sally, are country folk through and through who obtain game birds, pheasant, partridge and wild duck by helping out with their working dogs 'picking up the casualties' at local shoots.

I no longer shoot owing to a bad chest, but also to the dawning realisation that after so many invitations it would be churlish not to reciprocate... which as a pauper was out of the question. The beaters and keepers didn't seem to like my dispensing coins from my shotgun-shell coin dispenser rather than palming them a crisp note, and neither did I own a shotgun. I had to borrow one. And I certainly didn't look the part in my wicked Uncle Donald Cotton's dodgy antiquated Norfolk jacket, which he used to wear around the drinking dens of Soho, such as the Kismet Club, in order to build up the mystique of himself as a countryman and as if in denial that he was in the Metropolis.

Knowing my interest in, but conspicuous failure to 'live off the land', Mick and Sally last week donated a brace of pheasants and two mallard which I have displayed conspicuously by hanging them outside the cottage to advertise that we too are authentic country people who recognise the part played by blood sports in the preservation of traditional countryside features that might otherwise come under the plough: spinneys, ponds, rough field edges, etcetera.

It also improves the flavour. Game from the butchers or supermarket has never been hung long enough to become 'gamey' in flavour.

Therefore, I turned a deaf ear when Mick, who is a builder working exclusively with concrete foundations, parked up his tip-up truck outside our cottage and started working in the road with an axle grinder and power tools.

He was making a dickens of a mess with sawdust and wood chips, and intermittent grinding and mechanical whining noises.

Wednesday 16th

GILES: One of my guilty pleasures is watching *Neighbours from Hell*, a programme which in Mary's *Gogglebox* words is 'substandard on so many levels'. Often the TV neighbours will start off on a good footing on friendly terms only for a tiny incident, relating to noise or boundaries, to tip the balance towards adversity and suspicion.

We once attended a recording of *Gardeners' Question Time* in the Bouverie Hall, Pewsey. I was sitting next to my betters, of a superior rank, the Sandersons, when I asked the panel the bombshell question. 'My neighbours have built a hideous eyesore extension. Can you suggest a quick-growing evergreen climber that will help to camouflage it?' 'I hope your neighbours aren't listening,' said one panel member.' 'They are sitting right next to me,' I quipped. Philip Sanderson laughed nervously.

I used to laugh at the idea of twitching net curtains but I am getting more and more twitchy myself. Not least is my strong reaction to too many 'traffic movements', which I consider to be something associated with the suburbs. Another of my lost causes is the creeping suburbanisation of our rustic hamlets. 'Where are they off to now?' I demand as I hear the car doors slamming once again. 'They've only just arrived. You'd think they might want to stay in one place for more than fifteen minutes,' I harrumph to Mary who says 'get a life'. One of my greatest – Mary says most – irrational fears is that our neighbours might start 'tinkering' on their cars or vans in the street. STRICTLY NO TINKERING. Is this a sign whose time should have come?

My attitude towards tinkering she therefore deems negative and a good example of why I need a course in Neurolinguistic reprogramming. She can see on-street tinkering as a positive. As a resident of Northern Ireland who witnessed the Troubles at first hand, she sees the tinkerers outside as doubling as potential security guards or burglar deterrents.

The tinkering need only become a problem if I choose to let it do so. More annoying is the constant bombardment of helicopters flying too close to the village and crop sprayers dusting us with toxins. Oh, and the street lights. That is the project of a lifetime: to dismantle them and educate folk as to their inherent disadvantages.

It seems a shame that these stars which started their journeys so many millions of light years ago should be stymied from showing their glories a few seconds from earth by some council official in Swindon who is adhering to a street safety agenda and has consequently turned the village street into a Martian landing strip. The Campaign for Dark Skies is a peculiarly middle-class interest.

Thursday 17th

MARY: Phoebe has been acting strange, licking the sides of his plastic basket and later the eiderdown I threw down as a sheath between him and the windowseat of Room Two.

Yesterday the vet said he was probably confused by the dose of methadone he'd had for his cough.

This morning he woke me at three and wanted to go outside. We went downstairs and I opened the door to see a deluge. Phoebe walked out into it and then stood, stock still, resistant to my calls to come back, staring ahead. Eventually I had to go into the deluge myself and carry him back in. I wrapped him in a towel and we sat in silence on the sofa of Room Four. I rang Maureen the breeder. She said she thought Phoebe might have had a stroke. He's onto his third day of no food.

Phoebe going

<u>Friday 18th</u>

MARY: We wrapped Phoebe in a fur coat and he lay on the sofa staring ahead, but he drank only water and ate no food. In the garden he walked around and around and Lee, the *Gogglebox* sound man, said he thought he was looking for somewhere to die. We agreed to take him to the vet in the morning.

<u>Saturday 19th</u>

MARY: All these recent months I have been dreading taking fourteen-year-old Phoebe to the vet, leading him in there and asking for an injection that would kill him – a dog who trusts me. I could see how ill he was though and I hoped the vet might give him daily doses of morphine so he could glide slowly out of life like a canine Keith Richards.

We wrapped Phoebe in his zip-up dog's towelling robe and took him to the vet. He sat like a baby on my knee but I could tell there was little brain activity going on as his eyes were dull and misty and he didn't respond when other dogs, including a spaniel, came into the waiting room. He was breathing deeply and then he gave three deep, final breaths.

And then the door opened and the vet said, 'I'm so sorry to have kept you.'

But I wasn't sorry. I felt proud as I said, 'I think he's just died,' and we unzipped his towelling robe

PHOEBE THE DOG

and the vet took his heartbeat and looked in his eyes and confirmed that he had indeed died. The vet was almost as upset as we were.

But I was proud because, as Giles said afterwards, 'Phoebe was far more intelligent than we gave him credit for. Mum said he knew everything that was going on and he was so considerate that he even spared us the vet's bill by dying at will and he spared himself the indignity of being put to death.'

DECEMBER

Monday 12th

GILES: Phew! It's arrived! Last year, *Gogglebox* sent a Christmas bonus in the form of a hamper. It was most welcome and the anxiety of whether it would appear this year was heightened by Channel Four's rash and extravagant offer to Paul Hollywood to start a rival *Bake Off* – at £75 MILLION. Was it really as much as that? These figures put cottage-dwellers in a spin.

The whole mystique of a hamper is deeply retro. It's 'round the world in eighty days' stuff; it's Rudyard Kipling… it's a foreigner's idea of Englishness.

I would like to think that the hampers were made in England from sustainably sourced willow from Somerset withy beds, where generations of basket makers have eked out a living making panniers for hot-air balloons, and for the luxury-hamper market. Fathers teaching sons ancient skills from thatched hovels with hollyhocks round the door where the mother is scouring the front step and the baby is in a crib nearby with a black cat. Ahh! That is good… Mary has just confirmed by googling that the hamper was indeed made in Somerset by a family firm in their seventh generation of hamper-mongering, P. H. Coate and Son, whose fastest-growing line of business is wicker coffins, incidentally.

That would explain the astronomical price of The Epicure Hamper (£300), but women and children are no longer involved in the hand stripping of the bark of the willow, which is now done by noisy machine. More's the pity, for a neo-Luddite like myself. But this has taken the wind out of my sails, as I was just about to launch on a tirade against the global economy, assuming the hamper-making had been outsourced to China or Vietnam. Good for Fortnum's!

But, as Mary has observed, not only do I bite the hand that feeds me, I like to look a gift horse in the mouth. Like everything else, I have my reservations about the hamper, not least the tongue-in-cheek fruity language that accompanies the printed words on the labels – 'Your parcel of joy', indeed. 'We hope you enjoy the adventure.' Just as in previous years I will unceremoniously dive in, remove the superior spaghetti-like wooden shavings and use them for my compost heap – all heaps require layers of dry matter amongst the rotting veg – and line up the comestibles for some serious cherry-picking.

The Epicure Hamper contains a small proportion of inedible (my words) foodstuffs. One example is shards of lemon and orange peel, coated thickly in luxury chocolate. That is all very well but impractical; as with lemon zest in chicken fricassee, the reality is that there is simply too much spitting out required. The hamper also contains 'classic' marzipan fruits. These are replicas in miniature of oranges, apples, pineapples, etcetera, made exclusively of marzipan. I have never known anyone purchase marzipan fruits or even offer them to me in their house. In my judgement they should be confined to bushtucker trials along with crystallised fruit in general.

The 18-inch-high, dark-brown metal cylinders of luxury chocolate and walnut biscuits will be recycled as presents to aunts and uncles, in the full expectation that they will then be recycled by those aunts and uncles and used as presents for others they have failed to buy for in a continuous cycle of giving. The Germans have a word for a present that never stays with its recipient, because, although perfectly desirable in theory, no one actually wants it. It is called a *Wanderpreis* – literally a present that wanders.

Wot – no liqueur chocolates? We used to get tipsy on De Kuyper as youngsters but mayhap they are too plebeian for Fortnum's (mayhap is a very Fortnum's retro word).

Last year, Mary caught me trying out the crystallised peppermint creams late at night (we had run out of chocolate) and, not for the first time, I felt like Richmal Crompton's character, the eleven-year-old schoolboy, William Brown.

You see, my view was that the fact that I might have removed the odd cream or two from the bottom layer of the box in no way disqualified the whole from being recycled as a *Wanderpreis*. By the time, if ever, the recipient got to the bottom of the box, they would hardly notice, or assume it was a member of their own household who had done the filching. It would not be a mystery to which anyone with any sense would want to give time to the consideration of.

After all a few missing chocolates is a very small mystery compared to the big mysteries of BREXIT and TRUMP. Oh yes – and why no ale amongst the fine wines for those of us English gentlemen, like musself, who are allergic to the grape and prefer fine ales to fine wines. Wine drinking is for womenfolk.

MARY: The diatribe above is a perfect example of Giles suffering from what we call Ratnerlallia. Gerald Ratner, the director of the successful jewellery firm, when asked why he was able to sell his products so cheaply, retorted cheekily that it was because they were all 'crap'. The joke backfired and he had to step down. The shareholders were livid. Instead of Giles falling on the hamper with gratitude, he chose to start writing notes about what was wrong with it. 'Send an email, Mary,' he ordered.

'Ask is it possible that we can redeem the whole hamper for cash?'

Naturally I ignored this Ratnerlallia.

GILES: Cottagers of old would have fallen on the Dundee cake and Turkish delight like flotsam and jetsam from a looted ship. But sensibly I have wrapped these items for my elderly mother who has a sweet tooth but very little appetite. Christmas presents 'for less'. Good on yer *Gogglebox*!

280 grams of Salisbury Plain Honey took my interest as I read the blurb on the label:

> In summer we move some hives onto sites around Salisbury Plain. The army firing ranges on the Plain have surprisingly created a large area of wild grassland habitat, undisturbed except for the occasional explosion. Carpets of summer flowers spread for miles, scabious, sainfoin, vetches and numerous clovers producing distinctive honey.

I will bear that in mind when I'm having a quiet cuppa with toast and honey and the windows are rattling from the din of superguns on the plain. 'Occasional' indeed. Year round, more like, especially on damp days which, in Blighty, are year round.

When I first moved to a Wiltshire cottage I imagined the constant background noise would be that of chirping house sparrows – as supplied the soundtrack to every radio play and TV series set in the English countryside in the Seventies. Now sparrows are rarer than hen's teeth.

The thuds and rattles of guns on the plain and the clatter of helicopters are the reality of our country life. Occasionally a Chinook, on a so-called manoeuvre, comes thundering over the thatch shaking the brick-built cottage to its foundations and making us feel as if we live in Aleppo. But the wording on the honey label is wrong. The army hasn't 'created' the bioabundance (buzzword) of Salisbury Plain. It is one of the last remaining large expanses of land to have gone unmolested by farmers and provides the evidence of what nature will give us if spared the crucifixion of intensive farming.

The longer I live, the more it seems to me that conventional farming, so-called intensive farming and wildlife conservation are all contradictions in terms. Biodynamic farming, high conservation grade farming – now that's where they put the culture into agriculture.

MARY: Giles's description of the noise from the army's manoeuvres on Salisbury Plain is wildly exaggerated. They happen rarely. We hear occasional ominous dull thuds and see the occasional Chinook.

GILES: Just when you are feeling a bit post-prandial or liverish and need some old-fashioned Heinz salad cream or pickled onions to revive your worn out tastebuds, Fortnum's suggest you use their orange curd as a 'garnish for meat leftovers'.

No thanks. This leopard cannot change its spots. Lemon curd is acceptable but orange curd? Once again, the label is a bit of a giveaway, written in that characteristic, slightly fruity language that I imagine Simon

Callow speaking: 'Crafted in England from butter, eggs and oranges. Buttery, satisfying and awfully orangey.'

I am inclined to reply in my best public school mockney accent, 'You said it, mate!'

Orange curd?

It's like when I was a student at Harrow School of Art (Foundation Course), bedbound and breathless from bronchitis, I could just about stomach baked beans on toast. My sister kindly came to cook for me in the bedsit in Pinner where I resided. She duly presented me with a meal on a tray and I thanked her, but what a shame! She had thought fit to add mixed herbs to a tried and tested combo which needs no improvement, especially on the herb front.

'Start again Jax,' I wheezed. 'I can't eat this.'

Take this masterpiece of verbosity, from the label of the Fortnum's relish Anchovy Alchemy:

AN ARMADA OF SUPERIOR ANCHOVY,
WARM PEPPER
AND JUST A LITTLE DILL COMBINE
TO CREATE A TASTE THAT,
ONCE ACQUIRED,
DEMANDS
REGULAR
SATISFACTION

Not since Edward Lear have words been required to make shapes.

But a word in defence of the flowery verbiage that accompanies Fortnum's products. It must be remembered the store is selling a vision of England largely to Japanese, American and Chinese customers in search of that elusive *Downton* factor.

Friday 16th

GILES: Mary has forced me to come up to London for three days of Christmas parties which I cannot get out of. A kind friend, who normally takes in lodgers, but currently has a free room, was the host of one of these parties and suggested that, since our normal bolt hole is unavailable, we take advantage of the free room and parking (for friend of a resident) at only £10 a day.

It's a long time since I spent three days in London and it's bringing back fond memories.

For many years I have liked nothing more than to do a bit of moonlighting from my painting 'career' by helping London friends in their gardens. No assumptions should be made that, because of my age and encyclopaedic knowledge of horticulture, my contribution would be *designing* said gardens or ordering workmen about. On the contrary, I've always shied away from any position of authority.

What I like is the act of rolling up my sleeves and getting stuck into some pro-active clearing, pruning and letting in of light. It's the same impetus which makes Mary enjoy ironing – you get instant results and job satisfaction. I enjoy physically demanding work but my preference is that it should be mentally undemanding. I often wonder if my favouring of these infantile roles in the garden stem from the happy memories I retain of working during bob-a-job week as a wolf cub in the lane where I grew up near Keele service station in Staffordshire.

Observing this preference to always favour the downwardly mobile position, in contrast to her own upward mobility on the social scene, Mary has been known to call me a bob-a-job man.

MARY: Giles has always had a love of garden waste disposal. His ownership of estate cars – first a series of three Lada Riva Estates, then a seven-seater Peugeot, then a Volvo – has facilitated the removal of vast quantities of London-based garden waste, broken outdoor furniture and decades of plastic pots. So cathartic does he find the satisfaction of a decluttered garden that he was almost tempted to go into waste haulage as a profession. He has even considered having the legend 'Garden Clearance – no job too small' on the side of my car. But this sort of dynamism is not really his style.

GILES: It helps that I have an acre's worth of wild garden in which to process the London green waste by burning, composting or 'slow heap': a sort of laissez-faire composting where you dump stuff and it slowly decomposes to dark matter or 'humus' (as opposed to hummus, the foodstuff). The slow heap would provide a valuable overwintering site for hedgehogs if we had any, but we don't. The badgers have eaten them all.

But back to Shepherd's Bush and my tempo-
rary residence in Loftus Road where, ten years ago,
I was employed by the owner of another garden
in the same street. What made this wild, neglected
London garden a pleasure to work in was the insect
life: bees and tortoiseshell butterflies and hoverflies
were all attracted by a huge overgrown elder bush in
full flower resembling some half-hardy exotic from
sunnier climes.

In Wiltshire, the elder bush is viewed as a despised
weed, a dweller of drains and outdoor privies, and is
persecuted especially by the natives. But the status of
the elder tree or shrub has always been subject to the
vagaries of fashion, and currently enlightened land-
owners, fond of a little re-wilding, are finding themselves attracted to its wayward rampant growth.

The appeal is obvious when set against stiff
garden centre plants arranged in neat rows with all
the formality of a chess-board. Middle-class revivalists like myself read up old cottage herbals wherein
every part of the elder has been praised throughout
recorded history by Pliny to Evelyn as a medicinal
plant whose virtues border on the magical or miraculous. You could say it's the ultimate hipster's plant,
giving us elderflower cordial, elderberry wine and
the finest homemade flutes and pan pipes – the ultimate in authenticity. I would like to see bird-sown
elder bushes sprouting from every crack in London's
pavements, and that would have been a possibility
had we not strayed away from Europe.

A strong EU current of thought and opinion was well on its way to banning Glyphosate as a possible carcinogen. This is the active ingredient of Roundup, the world's most popular so-called harmless weed-killer and the cornerstone of GM technology.

Saturday 17th

MARY: Lovely to wake up in Virginia's warm, clean, bright house in the middle (up to a point) of buzzy London. Virginia is an agony aunt who has lost her weekly column on the closed-down print version of the *Independent* newspaper. She has been helping people in print for fifty years and, knowing that it's a vocational role, I had no hesitation in requesting a private consultation about a personal problem.

Virginia agreed, and I found it so helpful to thrash through all the agonies I am undergoing about having to sell my family home in Northern Ireland, which I co-own with my sister. We are not even selling it for the money – our eight-bedroomed house in a one-acre garden in the centre of a town. It was my mother's pride and joy, and my grandfather moved into it 102 years ago. But no one wants it.

I've had second and third opinions from people on my side, not crooks, and they tell me that no young people want to buy a 'period home' that needs work doing on it. Young people can barely change a plug, the estate agent said. It's been on the market for five years since my mother died. Finally my sister and I offered it to the next-door church at a cut down price, thinking at least it will serve a useful purpose to the townspeople, they can go in there and have counselling, meditation sessions possibly, prayer meetings and so on. But now we find out that, once the paperwork has been signed and the church owns the property, they are rumoured to have plans to bulldoze the house with all its lovely parquet floors and panelling and big windows, and use it as a car park. Last night an architectural historian was at Virginia's dinner and he and his wife begged theatrically: 'Do anything but don't let an Edwardian house be replaced by a car park. Anything would be better than that in a town which is already blighted.'

'What can I do?' I agonise to Virginia as I pace about her sitting room.

Virginia, with all her years of experience, is able to point out what had previously escaped me but once she mentions it, is blindingly obvious. 'All this is grief. You are trying to cling on to your mother, not to the house.

'Times have changed since your mother lived in that house. The town is not the town it used to be. She probably wouldn't want to live there herself if she had the opportunity to move into it now for the first time. You've worried about this house for five years. Your mother wouldn't want you to go on worrying about it.'

And of course she is absolutely right. I let the worry go.

GILES: The Uxbridge Road is the most ethnically diverse spot I have been to in England. Arabs, Afghans, Somalis, Yemenis, Lebanese, Pekinese, dirty knees so goes the playground chant. I used to read a massive book in my parents' library called *Peoples of All Nations*. Little did I know I would be meeting these very peoples a few decades later in my own country. Why the English kids feel they have to go abroad for a gap year experience is beyond comprehension when all the cultural diversity they could hope to experience is already present and correct on their own doorstep. Unless of course it's the sun and palm trees you are after.

Mary has gone out to lunch but since we have to go out again tonight in another gruelling round of pre-Christmas socialising, I insisted that I should be allowed to hide during the day in Virginia's spare room. I'm not alone amongst men whose hearts sink at the very thought of socialising. From watching so much TV, I can recall Bear Grylls describing his worst nightmare. Far from it being trapped in some sort of cave without food, light or water and surrounded by biting insects and snakes, he observed that his own worst nightmare would be to find himself stuck with a bore at a crowded London cocktail party.

Yet while Mary was processing old friends at the Chelsea Arts Club, here I was watching ring-necked parakeets from a window and sporadically letting myself out to spend this gap day immersing myself in the Heathrow Terminal Three-style crowds of the

Uxbridge Road. My aim was to see if I could integrate into this strange and unfamiliar world.

I set myself the challenge of finding a KitKat amongst the rows of halal butchers, Damascene restaurants, Sudanese travel agents and Jamaican barbers.

Eventually I was successful. An Afghani ironmonger has been cunning enough to spot this gap in the market and, as a nod to Western culture, has accommodated amidst the nuts and bolts, a small confectionery counter with KitKat centre stage.

As I proffered the cash, my attempts at affability were not so much rebuffed as ignored. The shop keeper continued to yabber away in Pashto or Dari on his mobile phone and with much gesticulating but no eye contact, he accepted the money and returned the one penny change which went into the Afghan helping hands charity box. Null points on the integration front. Not even thumbs up or a high five. Admittedly I couldn't do a high five myself – this leopard can't change its spots.

But over the road in Shepherd's Bush Market I admired the colourful packaging of olive oil, black peppercorns, pistachio nuts, Iranian dates and Turkish delight, all for less than in my local Wiltshire Co-op, and observed how much fresher and more appetising seemed the fruit and vegetables than on our own high street equivalent. The textiles alone were a feast for the senses and I even bought a pair of wellington boots for less (£12) and on exiting the souk-like market was recognised from *Gogglebox* by a woman who shouted 'Nutty!' Soon her dreadlocked partner had spotted me and I gurned for several selfies. 'Where's Mary, Nutty?' they asked. And I told them Mary was having an 'affair' so she was in a different part of London. We all had a laugh, or *laff* in the immortal words of Hyacinth Bucket. It's a go-to destination, far preferable to soulless Kensington. Yet now I've discovered the Uxbridge Road boasts a hipster café and a Polish shop which sells pumpernickel bread and kefir.

Ten years ago, I remember having to step into the road to avoid an excitable crowd of young men at the nearby Shepherd's Bush masjid. The prayer meeting was in full swing and once again I felt invisible. I had stepped into a parallel universe. A stranger in a strange land and unable to protest because the territory was theirs by dint of sheer numbers. Not that I expected them to part like the Red Sea, but an Englishman prefers not to be run over by an omnibus but to walk on the pavement.

In the intervening decade, a victory for common sense and race-relations has resulted in a prominent sign being erected: 'Please do not block the public pavement'. If we are to integrate on this over-crowded damp island, we must emulate the Japanese by being much more disciplined and more polite. We must robustly defend our values and not yield to zealotry. I once had a car sticker knocked up by the local printer 'say no to women bishops'. The printer really enjoyed the challenge – he photoshopped the head of a long-haired woman onto an image of a dog-collared vicar and had a large X through it, but my politically correct youngest daughter peeled it off, stating that if I parked the car anywhere near her student lodgings in Oxford's Cowley Road the Volvo would certainly receive a brick through the window. It was only meant to raise a laugh, but for her generation the only legitimate target left in Britain today for ridicule are the upper classes.

Sunday 18th

MARY: I paid an agony aunt favour back to Virginia. There was a giant duvet cover on her kitchen draining board. Virginia explained that it would take three days to dry it because it was too big for the tumble drier and for some reason her washing machine had left it sopping wet.

I suggested that as a treat for her I would take it round to the laundrette on the corner and put it in the giant tumble drier there. Virginia was amazed that such a thought had never occurred to her. I took it round and spent thirty minutes of bliss while it dried.

I have always loved laundrettes. They guarantee more happiness to me than a trip to a beauty spa would to another woman. First of all, there are the community viewing and bonding opportunities, the sense of real life and real talk. Then the sense of competence. These are machines that even I am able to work. Just slot the right money in the holes and ram the tray in. There is nothing to beat the satisfaction of tackling a simple job and doing it well. The duvet cover comes out bone dry after thirty minutes of my spying on the local women and men coming in and out and chatting to the laundrette keeper about what they are going to buy from the market for their Christmas dinner etcetera.

Tuesday 20th

GILES: I am twenty feet up an extending ladder which I have tied, for personal health and safety reasons, to the trunk of a Black Walnut tree, donated to my plantation by my brother Pip. I was about to cut a lateral branch that was as thick as my own leg as I felt instinctively that the vigour of the tree's growth was being diverted into this rival side branch and threatening to unbalance the original crown of its parent tree. I have got to the stage now where my thirty-year-old trees are telling me what to do on a telepathic level. The so-called Wood Wide Web has been identified by the German Forest Ranger and best-selling author Peter Wohlleben (*The Hidden Life of Trees*). The high winds on these Wiltshire prairies mean that tall brittle trees tend to be blown over. So I am converting part of my wood into thickets by cutting selected trees or shrubs to the ground which (fingers crossed) will promote rapid bushy multi-stemmed growth. The process is called coppicing and is at least as old as the Neolithic period. Not all species are suitable for this treatment but it is hugely satisfying work and quite addictive.

However, I would argue that restoring habitats on ecological principles seems an infinitely better way of spending my time than watching sport, drinking alcohol or going to lap dancing clubs as other men do. I love being outdoors I am in my element. Mary is in her element in a restaurant or cocktail party telling anecdotes to an appreciative audience (preferably those who are new to the anecdotes). Mary has a tendency to set the scene of an anecdote to an almost over-descriptive degree. I remember her Aunt Joan, in Dublin, asking her son Donald whether he had time to hear an anecdote about something which had happened in the bridge club. Donald, who was on his lunch break from work replied, matter-of-factly, 'Yes – provided you don't start it with the day you were born.' And I know the feeling.

Wiltshire seems dank after the contrast of multi-coloured, multicultural London. It was the worst kind of winter day: short, sunless cold and dark. In order not to be defeated by the winter you must force yourself outdoors. Hunting and shooting and the ownership of dogs who need walks are the means by which members of the countryman fraternity ensure they are driven outside whether they are dreading it or not.

How different my life might have been had I emigrated to Australia for my health.

Up here in the bare branches of the tree canopy wearing my camouflage jacket I have a bird's eye view of my wood and soon I hear the rusty gate hinge squeaks of a troupe of gold crested wrens. They are so tiny that they almost resemble Christmas decorations. It's odd that extremely small creatures are the least afraid of mankind. A blackbird or thrush would start in fear if you approached them, not so the gold crest.

Other branches offer me the spectacle of coal tits, long tailed tits, and wrens and robins which often hunt for food in packs.

Unobserved on my perch I spot Mary framed in the window of Room Two, where she's ironing. It's her way of relaxing. I just wish she wouldn't use white Irish linen table napkins as they enslave her in an endless washing and ironing treadmill and are quite unsuitable for *the way we live now*. What's wrong with kitchen roll?

MARY: Regarding kitchen roll – it's too much like having loo roll sitting about, but these hundred-and-something-year-old Irish linen napkins lend a certain distinction to the table. Unlike in my grandparents' day when people hung onto their own napkins, identified by their own napkin rings for day after day, and were therefore careful not to generate too many smears, I encourage my guests to use theirs with gay abandon. They stand up to any number of batter wash cycles. Holding and handling them is a sensual pleasure and the intricacies of their subtle design bear up to sustained scrutiny. Of all the things which are enjoyable to iron, table napkins offer the most satisfaction – especially when I wield the spray-on starch available from the hardware shop in Devizes.

GILES: My garden boasts bullfinches which, with the aid of my new Chinese manufactured binocular, resemble miniature parrots with exotic pink colouring. Since I'm the only local 'landowner' with dock plants – the others are too tidy-minded to tolerate them – I'm the only one to attract bullfinches which feast on the seeds so I have the last laugh.

I am a weed worshipper and Mary is really starting to appreciate teasels especially when the bees forage and later the goldfinches probe the seed heads.

There's time to think when perched at the top of a ladder which is gently swaying in a light breeze. Huge efforts were expended year on year in planting trees, but why didn't I just wait for them to arrive instead of doing it myself? This they surely would have done, as anyone who has seen trees growing on railway embankments can testify. No one planted them, they are wildlife. It was Richard Mabey who first pointed out that tree planting is an activity more to do with atonement for our warped relationship with nature than with anything else. That deep-seated sense of a fall from a state of grace comes from the fact that we were the first nation to industrialise our landscape and most city dwellers dream that one day they will leave the city and return to a country cottage with apple trees in the garden and roses round the door. On daytime television, this fantasy is packaged into a programme called *Escape to the Country*. Like most terrestrial daytime television it is a terrible thief of time.

Down to business, enough dreamtime. I spray the bow saw with WD40 and perform the undercut in order for the cut branch not to snag or leave a hinge of stripped bark. The exertion coupled with fear causes a trickle of sweat to run down my forehead. One of the disadvantages of hard manual work in a cold climate is this clamminess of cooling sweat which would burn off if I was cutting a Californian Redwood or Australian Wattle. How much longer must I live in a cold climate? The Englishman's lament.

Andy Martin, who is a professional local tree feller, speaks in hushed tones of widowmakers – beech trees with vast crowns which he had to fell in the Savernake Forest back in the 1970s. Trees have ways of fighting back their oppressors: dead branches fall in illogical trajectories, in such a way as to maim; and live branches, when split off from the main trunk can, when tormented by man, spring back in sudden and unpredictable ways to get their own back.

> Ellum she hateth mankind, and waiteth
> Till every gust be laid,
> To drop a limb on the head of him
> That anyway trusts her shade

December

Andy Martin derives adrenaline from his job – it's what gets him up in the morning. But nothing he does is in a hurry. 'Slow and steady' is his motto. I let my saw do the work in an easy rhythm back and forth; a splintering and then a cracking noise like treading on an icy pond was followed quite suddenly by a sound like a triple rifle shot as the huge limb obeyed the immutable laws of gravity. Landing on its springy branches it bounced and tried to nudge me off my ladder but I had outsmarted it by tying a safety noose.

In the still air the noise ricocheted around the vertical escarpment of the Downs and was echoed back by the gable ends of at least three brick cottages. Quite a racket all in all, causing some cottagers to exit their rear garden doors like so many cuckoos from cuckoo clocks to get to the bottom of what had made the unwonted commotion. To my satisfaction my camouflage deerstalker jacket – as preferred by hunters, supremacists and survivalists – gave me excellent cover, rendering me invisible.

Not so to Mrs Wood, who against strict protocol, flung open the unsafe upstairs French windows and bellowed, 'Stop cutting trees down, you cruel sadist! I liked that tree.' Ouch... why can't women shut windows and doors without slamming them?

Opening this particular window in winter is crime number one. A gust of wind might wrench it off its hinges in today's climate chaos. Furthermore, the same gust might carry the glass with it and even cause a beheading in the village, like the scene in *The Omen*. But more pertinently, Mary had interrupted my quasi-aboriginal deeply meditative man-time state, which at its best is like a waking dream. My sacred elfish woodland world had been shattered by the inconsiderate profane alarm call of my fish-wife who would prefer me to spend my time painting pictures on the grounds that she married an artist not a lumberjack! Fair enough. She's got a point but I have Dyschronometria, an inability to notice time passing. I often suggest we pop in to see my godson, Harry, at nearby Marlborough College but he's now 33 and living in Kenya and over all the five years he was at the college I only took him out twice because I kept thinking it would be better to leave it until we had better weather. I always think I'll start the painting in an hour or two but by then I'm tired.

Real gardeners work through the winter. Hobby gardeners only work in the summer. The job of letting sunlight onto my woodland floor and creating open sky where there was once a canopy is a case of correcting the condition of being unable to see the wood for the trees.

But I am now beginning to think that it may be the adrenaline of being on a ladder and doing dangerous tree work that I crave while I look for ever higher branches that 'need' my attention. Mary suggests that I may be getting some sort of legal high from this tree pruning, at the same time as overcoming my lifelong fear of heights (vertigo).

December

I once read, while in South Mimms motorway service station on the M25, from a novelty surname keyring, that my name derives from 'men o' the woods', and by the considerable power of suggestion, I may be fulfilling my destiny. But Mary cites the parable of the talents and says I am wasting my time in working as a labourer. She dismisses the mystic, Zen-like calm promoted by contact with the soil and by healing natural habitats to land damaged by pesticides.

JANUARY

Friday 6th

GILES: I enjoyed seeing something of my children over Christmas, but they both went off to separate events on New Year's Eve – Rosie goes every year to the Edinburgh street party – and now they've gone back to what I call their own little lives.

Since Rosie left the nest she has successfully fledged and, long ago, she stopped ringing in to relate blow-by-blow accounts of her daily life. She says this is because at the end of a day as a teaching assistant she is too knackered. Neither am I on Facebook or Instagram or Snapchat or Twitter so, to my continued bewilderment, my sister, who is on Facebook, knows what my daughter is up to before I do.

Both girls have inherited the socialising gene from Mary. When Rosie was at university we called it twentyfirsity, since she was constantly celebrating someone's twenty-first birthday. We hoped it would come to an end when she graduated but instead she is now constantly celebrating someone's twenty-second or twenty-third birthday.

I feel if I were able to find her number and ring her to tell her my own news – i.e., that there were not one, but two bullfinches on the nyger-seed feeder on a particular day I would inevitably get through just at the point when her Uber had arrived to take her to yet another party, and I get the sense that my news is irrelevant and slightly off-message and that I am holding her up.

But not content with parties she also attends After Parties. When Mary and I were young we were quite satisfied with the one party – we might go to one a month at most. Never mind an afterparty. We'd never even heard of Prosecco or pop-up magicians.

A few cans of Bulmers cider, 'Brown Sugar' blaring in a village hall, girls one end, lads the other, and cheese cubes and pineapple on a cocktail stick was good enough because, sadly, the cheese and chive dip got cigarette ash in it. So it was demoted to an ashtray.

MARY: This last entry is a typical example of Giles having Seancespeak – on this occasion he is channelling our pest controller Denis, who has just been round the attics laying poison. Giles never went to a party in a village hall in his life with girls at one end and lads at the other. But it's true that in our day people didn't have so many twenty-firsts. Neither Giles nor I had eighteenth or twenty-first parties. People were simply not so egomaniacal and narcissistic as they are today – a trend propelled by social media.

Unlike Giles, who has 'reservations' about almost everyone apart from around six friends, Rosie is supersocial and benignly disposed towards the whole human race. And Fleur sees successful party-giving as a genuine achievement as valid an art form as a painting.

Since I'm not on Facebook, Snapchat or Twitter either, I can't 'follow' them. But I'm better at knowing the right time to ring them. And also that Rosie prefers to text rather than speak on the phone. 'That way you don't have to take your eyes off the screen,' she says.

Giles could, of course, feel much more involved in their lives if he had an iPhone because then he could send them photos of bullfinches feeding off his nyger seeds and even be set up to follow them on Facebook, although I believe that like many of their age group they are now concentrating on other forms of media like Snapchat Stories instead. Unfortunately, though, I can't risk letting Giles have an iPhone as I know he would immediately start using it to document agricultural crimes committed in the neighbourhood, such as inappropriate tree planting – he believes the copper beech, being purple in colour, has no place in England's green and pleasant land. He would photograph tyre burning or film farm workers spraying pesticides on windy days and inflicting other ecological wounds on the landscape, and he would upload all these things onto trouble-maker websites. Like a rabbit trapped in headlights he would be sucked immediately into the websites of obscure anarchist eco-groups which promote sabotage and conspiracy theorists and that would be it, as regards socialising or painting, for the rest of his life.

This is why I've given him a pay-as you-go mobile. It's an analogue version with no more than £15 worth of credit in it at any one time as he can't seem to remember to press the disconnect button after he's made a call and he likes to leave it in plain view on his dashboard with the car parked in the village street and the windows down.

GILES: One person I can always get through to, and who always welcomes my call, is our trusty old friend from Yorkshire, Jo Farrell. She rings in herself twice a day to speak to Mary and I often pick up the extension when I hear through the floorboards that it's Jo. Today her husband Gerry, one of my best friends, was barracking her in the background so I asked to have a word with him about Rosie.

'She never rings me!' I grumbled to Gerry.

'Don't complain man, get a grip. You are extremely fortunate,' he insisted, 'in having somehow succeeded in producing a self-sufficient, well-adjusted adult. Unlike yourself. What's more she is the centre of a normal group of loyal and supportive friends of her own age.'

'A group of friends,' I reminded him, 'all of whom also seem to be indefatigable party goers who never tire of pulling silly faces in groups as they pose for photographs and then laughing at the results on their iPhones in scenes repeated up and down the country. Who never stop going to a party long enough to ring their aged parents. Congratulations! Indeed.'

'Giles,' he replied. 'Why have you started talking in those long and breathless sentences as though you're reading from an autocue?'

I told him it was partly because my voice, as my Jungian analyst told me all those years ago, is never heard. And on the rare occasions when I get the chance to have some contact with a willing listener from the outside world then I am going to jump at it.

'And also because I'm now very overweight. That could be why I'm sounding breathless.'

MARY: Both of our daughters have Apple Airbooks of superb efficiency while Giles and I struggle along with, respectively, an eleven-year-old Apple Mac desk top and a nine-year-old HP laptop. It's one of the reasons why I like to work on other people's machines or in the library. I find it so much easier to stare straight ahead at a big screen rather than staring down, and promoting a double chin, at a small one.

Saturday 7th

MARY: It turned out that Rosie was going to another twenty-second birthday party only eleven miles from here last night. She had no idea how close she was to home as her generation doesn't read maps and depends on sat nav to get them to places. (She once went via Swindon when travelling to London from Kent). With her friend Kitty she had intended to sleep in a car at the party site. This she told me before her phone ran out of battery as it so often does but, being a beady mother, I've also got the phone number of Kitty, so I suggested Giles come to collect them at 2 am as I (correctly as it turned out) had calculated that the charm of sleeping in the back of a freezing car together would quickly pall. Giles (who never drinks more than one beer an evening because his system 'can't process any more toxins than that') quickly agreed on condition I would go with him so he didn't have to do any of the thinking himself.

It was bliss to wake up this morning and know that Rosie and Kitty were safely tucked up in bed in the Pointy Room and that we could spend the day looking after them. Kitty had to go back to London after lunch but with any luck we can keep Rosie with us for another night.

Sunday 8th

GILES: Rosie and I are never happier than when either binge-eating my home-cooked spag boll, or binge-watching a Netflix offering on her Apple Airbook. After lunch and before supper, together we watched *Stranger Things* in two sittings while the wind howled around the cottage walls, only stopping for hot chocolate for sustenance.

When the weather gets better we will go cycling together through the country lanes that lead to the pub two villages away. First I will have to take the bikes in the back of the Volvo to be mended.

In the olden days, men like me used to know how to mend a puncture. Now, along with other workaday skills, like knowing how to put laundry through a mangle, we have lost these abilities. Or maybe we have lost the will to relearn them since we feel our time is better spent binge-watching.

We need to see the return of village shops and to have them supplemented by a workshop of skilled immigrants, who would happily spend their days just mending things, giving satisfaction, at the same time as training a British apprentice or two. The dream of a craft-based society was envisioned first by William Morris. A vision that subverts the dead-end, quotidian assumption that humans are here merely to consume or produce more and more shoddy goods destined for landfill, as the only legacy of their existence.

MARY: If I came to power I would bring back the village shop. In this village of fifty souls, at least twenty-five of us make a fourteen-mile round trip to Waitrose or Co-Op every day. Often we are stocking up on just one thing, such as tea or cigarettes. We don't have a village shop but there is one three villages away. When you ask the residents there if they patronise the shop, they air-headedly often say, 'No. Because it's too expensive. For example, teabags are £2.49 in Waitrose, but £2.70 in the village shop.' And so, in order to get that one item, they spend at least £3 on petrol to make a saving of 21 pence.

Under my rule the Big Four – Tesco, Waitrose, Morrisons and Sainsburys – would be responsible for the subsidy of a certain number of mini-Tescos, Waitroses, etcetera, in the centre of villages. They would just sell core products. They might not have enough footfall to match the giant profits they make in their mega-stores but they would be giving something back because each village would not only be spared the emissions created by twenty-five people making fourteen-mile round trips, the village shop is where a lonely pensioner can be sure of having at least one conversation a day. And the general gossiping about potential sightings of burglars or young offenders etcetera would do so much to reinforce community cohesion. Now that we don't bond at the church (I do, but only a handful of others from the village join in) we need a centre for communal interest.

Monday 9th

GILES: We are still feeling stuffed after the excesses of Christmas and this morning I felt a twinge of recognition when I read a shaming human interest story set in an Italian hotel.

'Greedy guests at hotel breakfast buffets are hard to stomach,' says playwright Alan Bennett. As an Alan Bennett-lookalike, I always pay attention to what the wry leftie has to say. At a Venetian hotel he observes, 'Some of the well-to-do guests can't wait to get the food back from the breakfast bar to their table, one young man downing a tumbler of orange juice en route and a boy stuffing himself with sausages before he even sits down.'

Reading this gave me an uncomfortable twinge of recognition. Back in June, while staying in Hotel Tornabuoni, in Florence, I had guzzled a chocolate croissant at the buffet breakfast bar. Impatience had overcome me while waiting for the toaster – a medieval-type instrument of torture which used a process akin to briefly waving a slice of bread past a three-bar electric fire, then twenty seconds later repeating the interminable process.

And yet Italians are the world's top designers of white goods, and have no difficulty churning out highly sophisticated working Ferraris, Lamborghinis and Maseratis.

In my defence, the hotels who run these bunfights, aka buffet breakfasts, are asking for trouble by cutting down on early-morning staff. If more waitresses were available, oafish, dog-eat-dog, and other churlish behaviour would cease.

I read in another paper recently that we all have a 'reptilian' part of our brain which serves to fulfil the basic functions of survival (not including higher functions like consideration, empathy or guilt). There is nothing like the sight of a large German lumbering towards the last croissant to excite the reptilian section in the brain of a nifty Brit like myself and see me outmanoeuvre him and grab it first.

To my generation free orange juice is still a treat, which is why I drank a litre's worth at that breakfast. It goes back to the days when the red tops discovered mountains of orange halves set out for the binmen at Gatcombe Park. It emerged that Princess Anne was squeezing, or having staff squeeze for her, dozens of REAL oranges for her morning glass of juice.

Back in the Seventies people had never seen excess like it. The story reignited stirrings of Republicanism in this country. It goes without saying that Princess Anne is the second most hard-working royal.

Yet we are not so different from cavemen, as road rage testifies. Feasting and tossing bones over our shoulders is part of our hunter-gatherer past. One mile away from our cottage is a hill fort where feasting would happen sporadically as a form of community bonding. Today feasting happens every day and the consequences of over-eating present a uniquely first world problem.

The continental breakfast is itself a mystery. A food–combining nightmare. Why cheese? Why salami and cold viands as well as pastries, prunes, yoghurt and choux? But we breakfast brutes are very suggestible. 'What is it there for' our reptilian brains ponder, 'if not to guzzle?'

Mary informed me, 'You're not supposed to eat it all. They have to have a variety to cater to different tastes and nationalities.' But then the camel's-hump part of my logic kicked in – shouldn't I stock up now in case there is nothing to eat later? What about all the refugees coming from sub-Saharan African via Lampedusa and now, allegedly, passing through Italy. Won't their presence trigger shortages?

Humans have not adapted well to a world of plenty. Mary likes reality programmes about Fatties and, while getting the fire going for her tonight, I noted one obese Briton being confronted by a table-load of replicas of exactly what he had eaten the previous week. The quantities alone resembled what had been laid out in Florence for one breakfast for sixty people. This denouement was accompanied by gasps from the Fatty of feigned astonishment and mock disgust. But also a puerile pride in his greed having attracted so much attention it had made him the focus of a television show.

Another thing, Mr Bennett. We humans are 'territorial' and even 'tribal'. A word rarely used in debates about over-population within the context of immigration. The sight of three Bavarian mountain men heading towards a pile of mortadella sets a panic button off in my head and I grab a bit – just in case.

'You hate mortadella,' Mary reminded me as I sat down with my loaded plate. 'You said a moment ago that it's the lowest form of processed meat. So why have you taken it?'

'In order to stop the mountain men,' I hissed, before heading back for some gruyère at the same time, and a plate of chilled strawberries.

It seems to me that too few nutritionists, dieticians and food doctors have sufficiently examined the psychological causes of greed, or the atavistic fear of famine, leading to yo-yoing. Feast or famine is a cliché. It was used in the plot of *La Bohème*, the opera by Puccini about starving artists in a garret, who at one stage break up the furniture to fuel the flickering embers in the grate.

With camel's hump syndrome I don't know when my next oasis may appear, so eat drink and be merry, for tomorrow you may die... in the western world more likely of a heart attack. For this reason most villages in Britain now contain a defibrillator machine. A sure sign of the 'Descent of Man'.

Thursday 19th

GILES: I took Mary to the station. She was going up to London to helicopter parent Rosie and sort out a bank statement problem.

An uncomplicated soul, Rosie once startled me by saying if she was run over by a bus tomorrow, she had already clocked up so much joy and happiness in this life that she wouldn't grumble. Wow, where did she inherit those positive genes from? Certainly not from my side of the family. She seems to live in the moment, not unduly concerned with past events or the future, perhaps that is her secret. Neither is she burdened with philosophical or intellectual questions of an existential nature.

Meanwhile, I must ring her to check that she purchased a protective case for her Mac Book Air, which I promised to pay for. Is the prefix 07783, 07883, or 07833? Either way, one of those people I have been misdialling is a very polite, endlessly patient Italian woman who repeats 'no problema' when I have serially apologised over a nine-year period. This was a sound reason not to vote for Brexit.

Friday 20th

GILES: Mary has arranged for me to have a memory test at our local surgery. She cites many potential disorders that her research suggests I could be suffering from and which need to be formally diagnosed. The shortlist includes a condition called fronto-temporal dementia, where one is deranged only some of the time. Today she handed me an article from the *Daily Mail* about conditions such as 'glass delusion' where the sufferer believes him or herself to be made of glass and Charles Bonnet Syndrome where the sufferer's clear as daylight hallucinations are caused by macular deterioration in the eyes, and the brain, compensating for the lack of action in the field of vision, broadcasts old material from the brain's memory bank. Surely this explains ghosts once and for all?

Mary says, 'I'm just saying you too might be suffering from some sort of condition which could easily be cured by a small medical intervention.'

But personally I have taken steps to save the NHS thousands of pounds by drinking only the recommended units of alcohol – indeed fewer. Local society hostess Louise Brewer took great exception to my referring to her fine wines (Petrus and Margaux) as units of toxins when she heard me ticking off Mary, who was clearly overstepping the maximum recommended.

Regular liver tests as part of a human MOT make sense on the basis that prevention is better than cure, since no one wants to end up like George Best, even if he did have an airport named after him. (NOTE TO SELF: must make list of airports inappropriately named in honour of drug abusers and drunks… John Lennon, George Best. Only two so far!)

I was enjoying *The Family Doctor*'s chapter on confusion and forgetfulness when Mary rudely snatched the thick volume from my lap. My sin? Guilty of being slow-witted and taking too long to turn the pages. Her sin is impatience, but as my analyst once said, my voice is never heard!

Mary started firing questions in a staccato manner: 'Have you noticed two or more of the following symptoms: change in personality, decline in standards of personal hygiene, difficulty in following complex conversations and instructions, and inability to cope,' she probed, 'with every day matters?'

'You haven't got to the bit where the patient thinks his body is rotting from the inside,' I protested.

In the months before sending me for a formal diagnosis, doctor's daughter Mary has dubbed the syndrome 'Variable Intelligence Disorder'. OR VID. For example, my habit of asking her where she is going every night, in the middle of the night. A question that so infuriates her that sometimes she turns on the light and starts working on an article, despite my humble apologies. 'Sorry – I forgot'. The memory test was part of a full MOT with a nurse at the surgery. She started by chatting amiably and mentioning the name and address of a man she knows in Kensington.

Then more chatting amiably, then the question, 'Can you remember the name of the man I mentioned earlier and his address?'

I might have known I was being set up for an ambush.

I remembered his surname and the area, Kensington, but had forgotten his exact address within minutes. I was told I got six out of nine for memory. Not good but not bad... fair.

More worrying is the number of TV programmes I watch which require no input of intelligence whatsoever. They could be a guilty pleasure, and not a medical condition as such. Do the programmes themselves lead to dull-wittedness, or was I dull-witted to watch them in the first place? *Neighbours from Hell*, *Bargain Brits in the Sun*, any winter sun programmes – all these programmes rob you of precious time, especially if you sit down in the afternoon. There is a remedy for these daytime time wasters: emigrate to Australia or California. You will get more daylight hours, and waste less time just trying to stay well.

Half an hour after the appointment the name of the man came back to me: John Brown, of 17, Thackeray Street. Kensington.

The doctor gave me a clean bill of health and I am now thinking that Mary's insistence that I am suffering from a progressive form of mental deterioration may be inspired by the film *Gaslight*, in which a husband creeps around the attic switching off lights, etcetera, to make the wife think she's going round the bend, in a bid towards getting rid of her by having her institutionalised. I am institutionalised already – the institution is called marriage.

Saturday 21st

GILES: Joined Mary in London. We have been invited to stay in the top floor room still currently unlet as our friend Virginia seeks a new tenant. I have an appointment tomorrow with Fleur to collect her from her flat in Notting Hill and take her to the James Ensor exhibition at the Royal Academy.

Mary has been telling me for decades now that a mobile is essential in today's fast-moving world, not least for the purpose of having personal telephone numbers stored and easily accessed. She has given me such a device but I keep making the mistake of leaving it in my drawer instead of keeping it in the car glove compartment.

How am I going to find my way to Fleur's rented flat from Westbourne Park tube station except by 'poring' over a bulky, easy-to-read larger print version of a London A–Z? As my mother keeps reminding me – what a shame it is that no one in my family has the patience or the time to take me through the step-by-step procedures towards digital literacy.

On the other hand, I sometimes feel interconnectedness is over-rated and leads to homogenised thought forms. Today Mary is 'ghouling' over recently posted pictures of our contemporaries, also empty-nesters, spending their children's inheritance. Be it whale-watching holidays in the Azores, or camel riding in the high Atlas mountains, or just simple, charming close ups of wild flowers in South Africa, people who have the time to 'curate' their own lives as if they were writing for Condé Nast *Traveller* are courting hubris like Icarus. If you have a primitive mindset like me and the peasants of southern Europe, you risk trouble through showing off in this way – e.g., by attracting the attention of the evil eye.

These show-offs never make mention of the dental hygienist's appointments, or the time spent trying to track down the expiry dates of MOTs or road tax now it's all gone paperless. They don't seem to curate images of themselves groping for coins in pay and display car parks.

There's a funny cartoon in *Private Eye* of a couple in a Caribbean beach resort taking a 'selfie' with the caption, 'Right, let's post that up on mylifesbetterthanyours.com'.

Sunday 22nd

GILES: Twenty-five years ago, despite battling with impecunity, I thought BIG for once in my life and purchased a day return flight to Paris, to see a never-to-be-repeated retrospective exhibition of my favourite artist James Ensor (1860–1949) at the Petit Palais. The complete works would be on show.

Just to be on the safe side, I telephoned the French cultural attaché's office in London to reassure myself that nothing could go wrong. 'Yes Sir, the exhibition is open every day of the week,' I was told.

Imagine my dismay to find myself in Paris surrounded by over-excited continentals chanting and letting off fireworks because it was Bastille Day. I approached the museum to find it closed. Even though it was the era of Lateral Thinking as promoted by Edward de Bono, in the absence of Mary with her legendary 'can do' attitude to problem solving, I couldn't think what to do.

I couldn't even work out the public phones. Where could one buy the little tokens, used in those days in French call boxes? Neither could I speak French because six months of living in Italy had driven my memory of that language out of my brain in favour of pidgin Italian. The prospect of the runaway costs involved in staying another night plus the cost of a fresh airline ticket defeated me. Rather than ask for help I opted to drown my sorrows like *The Absinthe Drinker* by Degas. I inwardly performed a Gallic shrug and can't remember how I passed the day.

When I rang the cultural attaché on the Monday to complain the exhibition had been shut when he had told me it would be open every day he retorted, 'But Sir, obviously it's not open on Bastille Day. Everybody knows that.'

It was fuel for my pessimistic philosophy that nothing is ever straightforward. Mentally I saw only problems after that incident, like the stereotypical plumber who shakes his head and says, 'It's much worse than I thought, and I will have to revise my estimate for the job.'

Was this the moment I invented the Wood family motto, 'There's no such word as can'? In this respect the traditional game of Snakes and Ladders, as training for life's little vicissitudes, involving no skill, only luck, should be on the syllabus for schools of all denominations. It would be a necessary corrective to the platitudes of the 'yes you can' positive but unrealistic brigade headed by Michelle Obama.

And so it was that, twenty-five years later, I prepared to make the superhuman effort to go alone by public transport to pick up my daughter and take her to see the small James Ensor show at the Royal Academy. Disappointingly, the forecast weather event of 'thundersnow' of January 2017 failed to materialise – we now have to experience winter vicariously by watching it on television in other countries.

I managed to make my way to Fleur's flat without too much difficulty. Fleur rings less when her life is going well. I know her mobile number off by heart and we have a lot to talk about. She, like me, feels ill at ease in the universe and like me she feels she is a 'special case'. She is also a highly talented artist with no skill for self-promotion, unlike Hirst and Emin. Correction, no inclination towards self-promotion.

She had told me forcibly not to stop in the street to check my jumbo A–Z, but to borrow Mary's mobile, as this would risk ridicule, or worse, being filmed as a relic of another epoch. 'DUH! No one carries an A–Z any more,' she protested. 'Just as no one buys DVDs or CDs any more, except you, Daddy.'

She was rather overstating her case, I thought. But then her life is one long psychodrama, an emotional rollercoaster which will feed in well to her chosen path as an artist. One only has to look at Kirk Douglas's portrayal of Van Gogh to see that all the great artists suffered emotionally, and the suffering nourished their creativity. This is the main problem with the light-weight work of Jeff Koons – he's clearly never suffered a day's setback in his life.

Anyway, Mary refused to lend me her iPhone for the trip to Ensor. She says it is too great a risk since I might lose it and all her work contacts are listed in there.

Timing in life is everything. Just as I like to avoid Cornwall in August for the quiet of September, this exhibition was even more depopulated than I could have hoped for (I would wish England's population to return to Elizabethan levels. Elizabeth I.) Three ticket booths stood empty. The cloakroom also felt like a private gentleman's club. All my favourite paintings were there. This decision to go in the last few days was spot on, with none of that jostling for position in front of masterpieces and trying to interpose oneself like a pawn on a chess-board.

God works in mysterious ways. Would trying to tick off all the Ensor works in one day in Paris twenty-five years ago might have been a bit like turkey and too many trimmings... indigestible? I pondered. Less is more I say. Now I had the bonus of a talented daughter in tow. There is nothing more agreeable to a parent than to impart their enthusiasms to a receptive offspring, provided they are not checking social media at the same time.

One of my favourite paintings entitled 'Skeletons Fighting over a Pickled Herring', satirised the artist's turbulent relationship with the art establishment of the time. I thought how lucky Ensor was to be born in an era when it was actually possible to *épater le bourgeoisie*. Now, no one bats an eyelid at pickled herrings or pickled sharks or unmade beds. Indeed, art buyers almost require to be shocked to reassure them that their investment will rise in value.

I noted in the blurb that Ensor did his best work before the age of forty, after which he merely repeated himself. I intend to do my best work after the age of sixty, in order not to repeat his mistake. Ploughing his own furrow as the 'first expressionist', what an achievement! Unfashionably, and to his credit, he stayed in the same place, Ostend, all his life. Like myself he believed that the real power lies in the regions, not in the capital. And, like me, he felt no desire to 'network'.

For some unknown reason Ensor is hopelessly underrepresented in British collections. All the more reason to get on Eurostar to Antwerp or Brussels, to over-eat mussels and chips, all washed down by trappist monk-brewed beer. Belgium produced Magritte, Ensor and the surrealist Paul Delvaux, to name but a few. Jonathan Meades did a wonderful

TV programme on the weirdness of Belgium and its artists.

Small to medium-sized exhibitions of lesser-known artists have enriched my life this year in particular. Nikolai Astrup was an eye-opener at the hard to get to Dulwich Picture gallery. Twenty years earlier Mary and I were staying in what was then an obscure fishing hotel, Hotel Mundal, at the top of Sognefjord, and I had put up my easel to capture an interior since the rain was stair rods outside, when another resident came to talk to me and showed me a book from the well-stocked hotel library featuring their national artist Nikolai Astrup, unknown outside the country. Now I was to see all his works in England – another example of the mysterious jigsaw puzzle which makes up life.

By contrast, any exhibition that involves queuing, booking, or waiting in the rain for, *nein danke*! I dislike the idea of being just another statistic. I would like to make a list of all the blockbuster exhibitions I have missed in my lifetime, most memorably the Tutankhamun exhibition at the British Museum, and the Matisse at the Tate in 2014. I am particularly proud of never having seen the film *Grease*.

But Mary insists there's no point to making such a list especially as I would 'take the day about it' through Parkinson's Law. I disagree. To boast of all the things I haven't done would counter that despicable trend to make a bucket list of things to do before you die.

HOTEL MUNDAL, NORWAY

Thursday 26th

GILES: It's well known that appearing on television adds nine pounds to your perceived weight and maybe more. It doesn't help that the chair that Mary watches television in is a wrongly placed reclining chaise longue designed as a bedroom chair for use in what was presumably a less frantic and more leisured age when she could have lolled back on it by day reading Trollope. It could barely be less flattering since in real life she has an almost normal body mass index.

Or had. Despite TV screens getting slimmer, neither of us is. Like a lot of folk, I enjoyed feasting over Christmas. The birth of Christ was superimposed on pagan meat-based, mid-winter feasting rituals lasting days and stretching back to the Stone Age.

We are fortunate to live in a time of relative food abundance but the future is all on a knife edge. Today we have gluts of ripe, ready-to-eat avocadoes delivered to supermarkets on a 'just in time basis' and issues like Trump and Brexit are leading to a surge in comfort eating. Is it no wonder we feast on viands like Henry VIII all year round?

And goodness knows what will happen now the Indians and Chinese have developed a taste for meat, because animal agriculture is the worst thing for the planet. I know because, as I have already mentioned, I've watched the documentary *Cowspiracy*. And it's not just the flatulence...

Personally, I love that too stuffed to walk feeling from festive over-eating. You have finished the pudding and brandy butter and now it's time to inspect the new-look Toblerone bars, in which, in a graphic example of shrinkflation, the spaces between the triangles of joy have got wider!

I got a shock at the doctor's surgery when I went for my MOT last week: the cottage scales had been lying. I was not an overweight 14.5 stone, I was a massive 15 stone. It is cause for concern, the days for laughing are over.

In my defence, most Britons (one third) are now overweight or obese, so it's up to my mother's in Wales for a two-week boot camp of vigorous exercise and calorie-controlled diet. The main problem will be mood swings, but then I didn't ask to be born so it's logical in a blame-based society to shift the blame for my portliness onto my mother.

The first evening's supper was a punishment plate of unseasoned mince with carrots. 'Where's the mash, Mum?' I asked. 'I'm very happy to do the mashing for you.'

But it transpired that there were no spuds, and nor was there even the standard rescue remedy of a Blue Riband snack bar with which to refresh my mouth from the taste of mince when my mother went out of the room. As every woman who has a son or husband on a diet knows, they WILL suffer from mood swings.

I have inherited a sweet tooth from my grandmother who made meringues and force fed me as a nipper. I also witnessed her going back to a chicken carcass and eating crispy skin which made a deep and lasting impression. I often tell Mary that my admiration for my grandmother is partly to blame for my inability to resist whatever tasty morsels are accessible to me. Being Scottish, my grandmother used to pronounce it 'tuth'. To my prep school, she used to send packages of fudge so delicious that I had to eat it privately in my dormitory for fear of other boys over hearing my Billy Bunter-style groans of pleasure and demanding some.

MARY: Giles often pins the blame for his greed on the fact that he admired his grandmother so much and she herself was very greedy and always, following the Sunday lunches she invited them to each week at 43 Whitmore Road, Stoke on Trent, 'went back to the carcass' after everyone's plates had been cleared away.

I usually respond to this by asking why, if he admired his grandmother so much, does he not try to emulate the more positive aspects of her character and lifestyle, such as the fact that she was a tireless worker for the public good (she was a consultant anaesthetist) instead of singling out for mimicry her one small fault – greed.

Friday 27th

MARY: With Giles in Anglesey, I've decided to stay in London with Virginia. For better for worse but never for lunch goes the mantra re the desiderata for a happy marriage. I would prefer Giles to be out during the day in order to give me mental privacy and to allow me to get on with my work. It's jolly hard to concentrate on the aforementioned when a man keeps coming to the door of my pop-up office (e.g., Room Two, the bedroom or even Room One – the multi-purpose room) to ask a seemingly harmless question such as, 'Where's the coffee?'

'In the place where it's kept,' I'm likely to reply.

'It's not there. You must have moved it.'

I leave my desk and lumber past him towards the place where the coffee is kept. Giles has an odd habit of standing in the doorways he has invited me to pass through so that I am prompted to snap, 'Well get out of the way then.'

To which he replies, 'There's no need to be uncivil.'

Walking into the kitchen to the shelf where the coffee is kept, I find the packet and hand it to him.

'Why did you think it wasn't there?'

'Well it wasn't there a minute ago. You must have slipped it back.'

'Why would I do that, Giles?'

'Just to make me think I'm going mad so you can get the upper hand.'

There is, of course, the other distraction of Giles beginning to speak to me from a room that I'm not in. Now that Gug is no longer in the cottage to act as messenger, it means I have to get up from my desk and walk towards the room from which the disembodied voice is emanating.

'Giles! If you want to talk to me then come to the room I'm in!'

'I'm a busy man. And I never have any idea which room you are in. This cottage is unmanageably big.'

Then when dear Phoebe was with us there were the regular bursts of barking to disrupt my train of thought. What had triggered it? Going downstairs, I would invariably find him standing on a windowsill in the television room barking furiously. But how had he got up there? Giles would have lifted him there and be grinning with approval as he himself skulked out of sight while Phoebe barked at the sheepdogs exercising in the opposite field, the shepherd's girl-friend firing tennis balls for them.

'Giles!' I would scream. 'Why are you making Phoebe bark?'

'It's very good for his lungs.'

But though I dream of him being out by day, I don't want him out at night. The cottage is too grim without him there at all. And particularly without the dog, now our beloved child substitute and all-round love object has gone to heaven.

So I've decided to stay at Virginia's till he comes back.

Saturday 28th

GILES: I rang Mary in London to dictate my article for the *Oldie*. She complained that it was full of Seancespeak and that she could tell I was channelling someone called Forbes I was at school with and not my own personality.

MARY: The problem with *Gogglebox* life is that we now spend at least twenty-five hours a week watching television. This means that not only are we not exercising during this period of enforced recumbency, but that the other 'work' I do as a writer and journalist and PR for the Caribbean region all has to stack up like planes waiting to land at Heathrow. In the few moments per day when I'm not working, I'm conscious of trying to fast forward the relaxation process before going to sleep and starting on the work again the next day. Hence the hand stretches forward for the pistachios and wine that might speed on that process.

I can see no solution other than hiring in another Gug-type assistant to follow me around the cottage and make sure I stick to controlled and sensible foods. It was the solution that worked for super-fatty Brian Wilson of the Beach Boys, who only managed to finally lose the absurd amounts of poundage he had gained by hiring two security guards to block his access to the fridge.

Meanwhile I can see on Instagram that ten of the rich people I know are at either the Viva Mayr clinic in Austria or at Landershof in Germany.

No wonder society is pyramid-shaped. We are all greedy but those at the top are much thinner than those at the bottom because they are the ones who can hire in personal trainers and dieticians to curb their excesses and issue praise or blame of the sort we all got used to as schoolchildren. Even in adult life, praise from authority figures keeps a person on the straight and narrow.

Sunday 29th

MARY: I communicate with Giles through emails as he can't work his own mobile to ring mine and to spare his mother the expense of calling my mobile from her landline.

We discuss the security arrangements of the cottage. I've placed Sandi at number two in charge. I don't cancel the newspapers or the milk since otherwise the delivery men get confused. Instead, Sandi at number two has the milk and leaves the post and papers for me on the table of Room Four.

Monday 30th

MARY: Went to Cath Kidston's sale in Portobello Road. I love Cath Kidston's floral print products although I do have oilcloth fatigue. Her clothes are just up my street but these days the skirts are knee-length rather than the mid-calf length I prefer. I bought a knee-length skirt which I intend to customize with elastic so I can wear it on the hip rather than on the waist under a Cath Kidston knee-length dress. The only one left was size 14 but I'm size 15. I don't understand why she doesn't do big sizes because after all her core customers must be bagwomen – she sells mainly bags – and bagwomen, like me, have too much stuff and eat too much stuff and hence we are overweight.

As I walked out of the shop and along Portobello, correction, sidestepped the various obstacles, I spoke to size 8 journalist friend Ruth who was ringing from the health clinic in Germany. She doesn't need to lose weight but she was having an MOT on her body and being taught to chew every mouthful fifty times before swallowing.

I got a text from our friend Syrah, the former cottage bed blocker. Syrah, an artist, has one of the last Chelsea studios. She rang to tell me she has just bought a double bed so Giles and I can stay there. She loves us because we remind her of her late father who was our great friend, Euan.

This won't be the first time I have referred to the dictum of Alexandre Dumas fils. 'The chains of marriage are so heavy that it takes two to carry them and sometimes three. ' Seventy-three-year-old Euan came into our lives twenty years ago. He lived seven miles away. His wife had left him and his two daughters were at university. Having met him through a mutual friend in the dead of winter we quickly accepted his invitation to move out of our freezing cottage and into his overheated hilltop farmhouse. We moved in with the children then aged three and nine – they loved it because Nunu, as they called him, had a telly in those days and we didn't. Nunu only had two videotapes – *The Sound of Music* and *Charlie and the Chocolate Factory* – but we were happy to watch them again and again. Euan himself would always watch *The Sound of Music*, booming along in his excellent Frank Sinatra baritone. At the end, when the hard-hearted Captain von Trapp realised how proud he was of his children the tears would roll down Euan's cheeks. 'Ah, the eternal verities...' he would say.

We quickly both fell in love with this 'vintage Briton' whose views were so wholeheartedly unacceptable that even our other friend and neighbour, the writer Robert Harris, was not offended by them but instead fascinated by this embodiment of living history.

'The working classes are always in,' Euan would observe. 'Otherwise the plot of *The Bill* wouldn't move forward. When the police come round to interrogate a suspect he's always *in*,' he said, tapping the table with his forefinger to emphasise the point. 'If they were looking for me I might be at my Club, the Beef Steak, I might be at my hice [sic] in the south of France, I might be lunching with the Mannerses. But the working classes are always *in*.'

But it wasn't just the vintage attitudes, there was the old-fashioned civility as well. Giles was keen to imbibe from Euan's distillation accrued over a lifetime of courtesy. 'I notice that you always stand up when Mary goes into or out of the room?' said Giles. 'Is it absolutely necessary for me to do it, like a jack in the box?'

'My dear fellow, at the very least you should shuffle in your seat as if intending to rise,' he commanded. 'Women, particularly wives, like it.'

Tuesday 31st

GILES: Staying with my mother in Anglesey always offers me a chance to win back some mental clarity. No mobile telephones go off, and the landline, which rings rarely, is never for me. Moreover, my mother, clutter-phobic to a fault – she once sent the contents of her loft to the dump just to facilitate the entry of the men who had come to insulate it – has a manageable amount of photo albums and a manageable number of well-read books on her shelves.

Picking out one of these I found, interleaved within it, a letter written by me in the mid-Nineties. I found I had written that, as parents of two small children, Mary and I were locked, like Inuit, into a daily struggle just to survive. We were both too tired to read *Solve Your Child's Sleep Problems* and yet our newborn woke every thirty minutes throughout the night. I observed that the time seemed to go by so quickly that the children would be at university soon and I couldn't see my way clear to having four hours spare to read the book before then.

Mary then wrote a section of the letter telling Mum that it was she who eventually set aside time to read the book. 'Rosie stopped crying and started sleeping like a log the first time I put the advice into practice. In short it is this: put the child to bed, wait outside the door while she cries first for five minutes; go in and check she's all right but don't cuddle her. Wait outside the door while she cries for ten minutes; go in and check she's all right but don't cuddle her. Wait outside the door for twenty minutes – ad nauseam.

'The point is that the child eventually realises that she has not been abandoned but that it will take double the amount of crying to bring you back each time and frankly they can't be bothered.'

Mum, like Mary's mother, was amazed at how our generation of parents put our children first. It was not the same in her day. Rosie's godmother Lucie asked her mother, 'Did I cry a lot when you put me to bed as a baby?'

Lucie's mother shrugged and shook her head. 'I don't remember,' she replied unguiltily. 'Your bedroom was right at the other end of the house so we couldn't have heard you anyway even if you were bawling your head off.'

How on earth did Mary and I get any time to ourselves in those days? The simple answer was we didn't. I used to be able to talk to her in the days when I drove her to and from Waitrose but then she got a mobile and after that was talking to colleagues on it. Once her French friend, Variety, who she had known when she first arrived in London from Northern Ireland, came over from Paris to see the cottage for the first time ever. She asked Mary what had drawn her to this part of Wiltshire. Mary, who worked, in those days as in these, as a frantically busy freelance journalist handed her a copy of *Country Living* magazine and suggested that Variety read an article by Mary on this very subject. She said that she was too busy to tell Variety herself and this would save time by putting the whole story into a nutshell. I remember Variety's face. She was appalled. 'But I don't want to read an article about it. I want you to tell me.'

Another survival tool of Mary's from those days came back to me as I flicked through Mum's old photo albums. Hers was the generation before digital and she went to all the trouble and expense of printing out the photos and putting them into albums. In one of the ones of Mary from the mid-Nineties it was clear to me that she was wearing rubber ear plugs as she posed angrily for the photo.

'Look Mum,' I showed my mother. 'Those were the days when Mary wore earplugs so that she couldn't hear my point of view if she thought it was going to differ from hers.' Mum, who never wants to take sides, and especially not retrospectively, made an enigmatic response and then changed the subject.

But I remember at the time accusing Mary that in the one crude gesture of wearing earplugs, she was rejecting 'civilised and reasoned discussion in favour of a new post-feminist Neanderthalism'.

Discussing it with Mary that night by email she replied that it was the only course of action open to her during the sleepless baby months. 'I was so tired that I was likely to over-react to anything provocative you said. Since you found it devilishly tempting to be provocative I took pre-emptive action by wearing the earplugs so I simply wouldn't be able to hear what you said and thereby sidestepped being annoyed by it and having my energy drained further.'

FEBRUARY

<u>Thursday 2nd</u>

MARY: Virginia had a dinner party which I loved. Afterwards, when I came upstairs, there was a sad email from my sister detailing all the stuff the furniture removal men will take from the house in Ireland tomorrow, which will start trundling its way over to Wiltshire. So the gloomy ancestral Victorian portraits of unidentifiable family members in their gold-alike gilt frames will also make the journey but they won't find wall space. They'll have to go into the attic. I couldn't possibly throw them out, that would be so disloyal. Yet I can see that for Giles it is illogical for me to keep them.

Twelve years ago, however, when our friend Euan, then eighty, decided to move out of his house in Wiltshire and set up shop in Cornwall with his sixty-three-year-old girlfriend, he rang us drunkenly one day to say that he was filling a skip and we were welcome to come and claim anything we wanted before the lot went to the dump the next day.

Giles grumbled for one hour before we went and for the whole of the thirty minute journey there and the thirty minute journey back, to say nothing of the one hour we were present at the skip. 'I have no further use for these,' said Euan as he tipped a cooking vessel full of black-and-white family photos into the skip. I seized them. They were of absolutely no relevance to me but I knew they would be at some point in the future to Euan's then twenty-two-year-old daughter Syrah.

And indeed they were. Years later she greeted them as though they had been buried treasure unearthed and they are now amongst her most cherished possessions.

And yet Giles constantly tells me off for hoarding.

GILES: Why, after a week of coastal walks, chopping wood for Mum's wood-burner, substituting Medjool dates for Snickers and watching the portions, haven't I lost any weight but remain stuck on 15 stone?

What may have happened, it occurs to me, is that Mum only eats a boiled egg per day. Like a lot of octogenarians, she has a sparrow's appetite. My love of gourmet meals prepared from scratch, sourcing local and traceable regional delicacies, has not improved her appetite. After a few desultory mouthfuls she has been secretly shovelling her portion when my back is turned onto my plate in a behavioural pattern that might be dubbed 'granorexia'. In order to lose weight I must return home to Wiltshire. No son should try to return to the paradise of childhood once he has flown the nest – you only have to look at what living with his mother did for Norman Bates of the Bates Motel.

Friday 3rd

MARY: Reluctant as I was to return to the cottage in this cold weather, in the wake of the death of a village elder who we've all in the village known and respected for at least thirty years, I want to bond with my village friends. Also, the girl in the beauty salon in Marlborough had told me she had an appointment free and could glue on some semi-permanent eyelashes for me.

Saturday 4th

GILES: The supermarkets have allegedly run out of iceberg lettuces and other out of season veg like courgettes and aubergines. The crisis even made the *News at Ten*. A good thing too, muttered the seasonal veg snobs, who had a field day preaching the dubious pleasures of turnips and root vegetables. It got folk thinking a tiny bit about where their food came from.

Bad, icy and wet, unseasonal weather has ruined crops in the Murcia region of Spain. Iceberg lettuces, the staple of many prawn and bacon sandwiches are in short supply, and fetching high prices at market as a result of the crude economics of supply and demand.

Supermarkets boast about everything arriving on a 'just in time' basis. And here perhaps was a little taster of the hiccup caused by climate chaos widely predicted to disrupt routine agricultural operations in the near future.

Mass hunger cannot be cured by a Snickers chocolate bar. It leads to riots and murder. The reptilian instinct of our friend Gerry kicked in when he was particularly hungry at a Chelsea dinner party where most of the fellow guests were fresh from their jobs in the civilised art world. Gerry's plate arrived with a small helping of longed-for chips. When his wife's hand reached forward to nick one, instinct caused him to stab it with his fork.

Gerry was mortified by the reaction of those around the table who were not quite so hungry as he was. Luckily he had not drawn blood.

The Dinner Party. An agony for some men, is for others, the highest expression of a civilised person. They go against my gut instinct – so to speak – but they are what Mary lives for.

Friday 17th

MARY: To a pre-half term concert at my goddaughter's nursery school. I never fail to sob my eyes out at school events. Not gym display, of course, but anything to do with singing and fluting little voices. I really am mawkish by nature.

Giles, however, remains impassive in the face of all displays of emotion, even extreme ones. Once an American friend, Shirley, burst into tears as she told us she had concluded her relationship with a mutual friend of ours. It was for the best possible motive but it was very upsetting, not least because it would mean an end to our socialising together as two couples. I cried, of course, but looking at Giles's poker face Shirley assumed his disapproval. 'Don't hate me, Giles!' she cried.

'I haven't got the emotional range,' came his measured response.

(Those were the days before he would have been diagnosed as on the autism spectrum rather than just as an old-fashioned, stiff upper lip Englishman.)

GILES: I was very fond of Shirley but she was a self-admitted caffeine-addict (a condition I identify with myself). Shirley's caffeine intake (a half litre of black per morning) meant her life was a constant melodrama. I always felt she was channelling Barbara Stanwyck as a woman at the end of her tether in *Double Indemnity*, whose breathless and compelling performance made every utterance sound as though she was clinging onto a cliff edge. Even the most pedestrian plodders could be affected by this intense American woman, but I could never really take Shirley seriously.

MARY: I think the most emotionally draining of all school experiences took place during an old boys' reunion at Giles's former prep school, Heronwater in Denbighshire. The event came about because one old boy had written around the others alerting them to the fact that their popular former headmaster Keith Gaskell, known as KAG, was about to be ninety and suggesting those with fond memories of the school send cards.

So happy were the memories and so enthusiastic the Old Boys that KAG received so many birthday cards on his ninetieth he actually died from the excitement of opening them.

Old boy passions for the school clearly ran so high that an Old Boys Reunion was arranged. I had to force Giles to go. I was fascinated to see myself this magical land where he'd been so happy from ages eight to thirteen (unlike the hapless teacher Paul Pennyfeather in *Decline and Fall*). Seventy or so old boys got permission to assemble at Heronwater and we found that, although the school was now a Christian retreat, spookily the decor had remained unchanged in the thirty years since it stopped being a prep school.

The old boys looked around the long bounds, the lakes, the dormitories, the libraries and the dining room where silence was compulsory during puddings as there was enforced listening to a 78" of classical music on a record player.

At the end of the afternoon, the old boys filed into the school chapel for a service of thanksgiving led by an old boy who had taken holy orders. The latter now suggested they pray and, while so doing, call out the names of other old boys, now dead, who might have stood shoulder to shoulder with them in that chapel for five years or so of their boyhood. There was a silence. First one man called out a name, then another twenty or more names echoed around the chapel. The wives were helpless with emotion, yet none of the prep school old boys shed a tear.

'You see,' said Giles, putting a manly arm around me. 'Even with all the oestrogen in the water supply men are still the stronger sex.'

Sunday 19th

MARY: Those men we know who were of the age to do National Service often remark that the forced tidiness, and the compulsory requirement to have a place for everything and everything in its place, stood them in tremendously useful stead for the rest of their lives. How I wish, now, that some sort of punishment, even mild corporal punishment, could have been meted out to me in early life as a way of training me to be tidier.

I do spend a lot of time each day looking for things but then I've got a lot on. Five different jobs, all done from home, endless ironing, mending and books to read and review, make up, and, of course… my mobile. It all adds to the domestic tension, especially since there is no mobile signal in the cottage and therefore no way of ringing the phone to find out where it is – though I have installed an app called Time Talker which drawls out the time in an American voice once an hour. I can always fall back on that by standing in each of the twelve rooms by turn as the hour changes.

The difference between Giles and me is that while I am looking for a multiplicity of things, he looks for the same things each day. His car keys, his wallet, his asthma inhaler and his cufflinks. Oh, and the coffee and the milk and butter and other things that he calls me down to find for him when they were there right under his nose all along.

'Why can't men find things that are right under their noses?' I asked him today.

'Because women can find them for them...'

Thursday 23rd

GILES: Freak weather again. Alarming bulletins about how Storm Doris is rampaging through the country. I insisted Mary cancelled her 5 pm appointment with her financial advisor, Mr Money, as there were rumours of fallen trees en route to London and I had agreed to drive her to his office, although I would not have gone in. It was a triumph for common sense: Mary rescheduled the appointment.

MARY: For some reason, Giles resents my visits to Mr Money, and always declines to accompany me. He is cautious about small expenditure – always going for second-class stamps for example. Yet he prefers not to confront the larger financial issues.

Giles's recognised talent and unique artistic vision of the world seems to leave no room for the co-existence of a financial vision – unique or any other kind. For this reason I was happy to see my advisor alone – 'better one fool than two' as the Irish saying goes.

I had planned use the audio function of my iPhone as usual for our conversation because, although we both know I won't be able to grasp what he is saying, I like to think that comprehension will sink in later when I play the tape back at home. In fact I will still be none the wiser. All I have to go on is the knowledge that this advisor came recommended by the 'last Gent in the City' Lord Rockley, circa 1990, and that when we passed our friend Cyril onto him, who has surplus cash to 'play' with, he performed miraculous services – not least setting up a separate savings account for Cyril which he clean forgot about until ten years later. Mr Money refreshed his memory about it and it yielded enough money for Cyril to move from a small cottage to a grand seaside mansion without a new mortgage.

GILES: The reason I don't like seeing financial advisors is that they are fantasists. Mr Money knows that I can earn three thousand pounds from a painting, which takes me a month. He then does the 'math'. He extrapolates that there are twelve months in the year and calculates that since a painting can be sold for three thousand I can therefore earn thirty-six thousand a year.

The reason that I can't do more than one painting per year is that the huge forces I need to produce a painting require months of what I call recharging of my batteries, which involves coastal walks in Anglesey, contact with the soil and a period of fallow creativity to build up the supposed creative appetite for the next great effort.

I try to do my bit by husbanding scarce resources in imaginative ways. For example, I prefer not to use the windscreen wipers at fast speed, even during storm conditions, favouring the slowest operational mode in order to avoid wear and tear on the windscreen wipers and the unnecessary expense of having to purchase replacements. This is difficult as sometimes the Volvo has a mind of its own and likes to override what it sees as the less competent driver in a chilling reminder of what the future will be when we have ceded control to artificial intelligence.

MARCH

Friday 3rd

GILES: Patrick, the proper carpenter, came round yesterday while Mary was in London. He sized up the garden shed, which we've decided to refurbish rather than trying to build a graddexe (the new word for a home in the field for a Generation Rent graduate 'child' who can't get onto the property ladder).

We both like the look of bicycle-riding, six-foot-five-inched Patrick who, at sixty-eight, with a bald head, grey beard and always dressed in a boiler suit with a bobble hat, seems to be an old fashioned type who knows how to do things properly. We have already seen him about the village repointing stones and building front steps, laying damp proof courses and generally being a jack of all trades, which suits us very well. I believe he is the same generation that might, like me, have read *Zen and the Art of Motorcycle Maintenance* by Robert M Pirsig, *Future Shock* by Alvin Toffler or Carlos Castaneda's trilogy.

This book is all about rejecting the throwaway society and Patrick says he wants to reclaim the existing wood, repairing everything, making do and mending. He is even talking about reusing the old window frames. He rails against the heresy of built-in obsolescence and globalisation which sees us all as no more than passive consumers or producers. I have been quick to exploit this philosophy by asking him to repair two bicycle punctures and a punctured pneumatic wheelbarrow tyre. Why oh why can they not produce a wheelbarrow with a solid rubber tyre?

Saturday 4th

MARY: This morning Giles told me that he had ordered Patrick to put in double-glazed windows. Giles then, having had too much coffee (a Polish variety bought in the Uxbridge Road, which Virginia warned him might be at least half made up of ground-up Polish acorns as it was so cheap at £1.30 a packet), wouldn't tell me whether he has ordered revolting UPVC-coated aluminium double-glazed windows of the sort that seal in foul air (sold under the catchphrase 'say goodbye to external decorating') and cause microbes to flourish, or attractive ones of the type used at formerly freezing Wiveton Hall in Norfolk, which consist of a panel of almost invisible Perspex that screws onto the window frame in winter. These are referred to as secondary glazing. And are the sort that would have been popular with Tom and Barbara in the Seventies sit com, *The Good Life.*

'It's a no-brainer that we should have double glazing,' said Giles. 'We are talking about a wooden shed in the teeth of the gales coming off the coldest windswept prairie in Wiltshire.'

'But what *sort of* double glazing?'

'I don't know which sort he's doing,' said Giles. 'Why don't you ring him and ask him?'

'But you were physically with him yesterday. Why didn't *you* ask him or, at least, tell him we didn't want them in bad taste? And how much did he say it would cost?'

'I'm sorry Mary but I'm overstretched as it is. I'll make myself available to these people you have commissioned to do your various fantasy projects but I can't get involved in the details. As Philip Wetton [a polyglot, former diplomat neighbour] says "*Ich bin leider überfragt*" [I'm grossly overquestioned].'

With picturesque shepherd's huts on wheels (dimensions six feet by ten) costing £16,500 I dread to think that even a 'cheapo' garden shed is going to turn out to be unaffordable.

I think we may as well take out a loan and have a proper building made. We might as well use credit to do it before we have made the money rather than after we have saved it up, which may well take us up to death stage.

GILES: Mary is not a believer in deferred gratification, the chosen method of behaviour opted for by our parents' generation, though many in my generation, including Mary, are opting for deferred punishment with years of repayments stretching out ahead of us. In turbulent times such as these, the Woods have traditionally battened down the hatches and harboured meagre resources. I can save twenty pounds per week by giving up chocolate and crisps. Also, by personally choosing the cheapest available materials for the garden shed, I can monitor the runaway costs.

MARY: So I am none the wiser re the cost of the refurbished garden shed or what effect Brexit will have on my tiny savings. All I know is what happened the last time that Giles was 'clerk of works' when we had our extension built in 1999. In those days, I had a little office in an outbuilding attached to the Old Rectory further along the village. Our friends, the Sandersons, had moved in 1985 when the previous occupants went to heaven. They let me the office at a peppercorn rent and I went to work there each day. I had just been suffering from Legionnaires' disease and was entirely unfit for any purpose other than writing articles. Giles spent his days winding up the carpenter of that time.

GILES: The result was Geoff's legacy of passive aggression in the form of booby traps around the cottage. There are attic trapdoors that have lived up to their name, e.g., if you push them their unnecessarily heavy weight is designed to trap hapless knuckles and fingers. The cottage window seat is so heavy that only Geoff Capes could open it using two hands.

He built a cupboard to house my size-ten shoes but it's only big enough to fit size six so they always have to be at an angle rather than in satisfying straight rows, and he built a bedhead in wood which he tried to screw permanently into the wall so we could never move the bed to a different position in the room. He snuck in MDF where we had ordered elm and he fitted the lights with painful metal stalks which hurt your hands when you tried to flick them on.

All by way of leaving his legacy and having the last laugh.

<u>Sunday 5th</u>

MARY: The weather was good but even had it not been, Giles would have spent the day in the garden as usual. It is colder at night and he lit a log fire.

We often don't even look at the schedules on Saturday night knowing they will involve Nuremberg Rally-type hysterical mobs, shiny floors, flashing lights and irrational cheering, but Sunday nights are different, what with the soothing *Countryfile* invariably followed by something involving David Attenborough, Chris Packham or Ray Mears. Different for Giles, that is. I'm usually processing a chair full of newsprint while he shouts 'Look Mary! Look!' every forty seconds or so.

GARDEN SHED

GILES: The new natural world photography available since the arrival of drone camerawork is mesmerising. I can never get enough of glacial terrains or the Australian bush. I probably watch slightly too many news and current affairs programmes, I admit. Like my father who stayed up every night to watch *Newsnight* in the days of Paxman, I feel that just by watching I am somehow participating myself in the corridors of power. Although our television screen at 21 inches is roughly a third the size of that watched by most other Britons, don't forget the room itself is only 75 inches high and 144 inches wide, so I find myself powerless to resist it.

Friday 10th

MARY: Yesterday, Giles and I attended the sixtieth birthday party of a magazine mogul we've both worked for on and off during the last thirty years. Giles, dressed in his Austrian version of a Nehru jacket, complied with the dress code 'Black tie or similar' and afterwards admitted how much he had enjoyed the party. I'm thinking that he's definitely becoming less reclusive despite the amount of grumbling he does about social events.

Sunday 12th

GILES: There are times when our marriage enters such a tunnel of absurdity that the TV science fiction series *The Twilight Zone* comes to mind. I can almost hear the twangling, discordant music which accompanied it. Often a power struggle is involved, and one person is seen to bulldoze, Trump-like, their own agenda through the niceties of marriage. The ideal of marriage as being an equal partnership of two stakeholders seems to be kicked into the long grass as the battle rages.

Gug Six, the twenty-two-year-old Mary has recently been employing as a researcher-cum-factotum, has sat through many of the blood-curdling rows with a wide and appreciative grin on his face. He remarks that whereas rows in his own family result in the participants often sulking for days at a time, only thirty seconds after Mary and my rows have reached their noisy climaxes we are amiably discussing what we are going to have for supper that night or laughing over a 'lookalike' in one of that day's newspapers.

Mary keeps a file of newspaper photographs of fairground mirror style grotesque versions of some of our nearest and dearest friends and relations. We both rue the day when we failed to act while having coffee one morning in Oxford's covered market and saw a real-life version of one our best friends who has a high domed forehead. Let's call him Dirk. Dirk Two's forehead was double the size of Dirk One's. His facial features were otherwise exactly the same as Dirk One's. Neither of us had a camera at the time (it was the days before they were extant in all mobiles) and we couldn't capture the evidence that

Dirk was not just a one-off human being – Dirkness was a *condition*.

Now crazed with grief for our lost dog Phoebe, Mary has seen fit to enter into a conspiracy of three against one – herself and our two daughters versus me. She has made an appointment to meet a Tibetan Spaniel puppy breeder at the South West Tibetan Club show in Grove, near Wantage. 'You cannot be serious,' I hear John McEnroe's voice whining in my ears. I have just destroyed the dog fence and given several dog bowls to the charity shop, and I have fed the remainder of Phoebe's dog biscuits to local sheep. I do not intend to erect another dog fence for at least another decade – if we last that long, Trump willing.

My father, Godfrey, was also of the belief that his family were plotting against *him* in nefarious ways but he tended to lack evidence – primarily because we weren't. I, by contrast, have proof of foul play.

For, once in a blue moon, I actually listened this morning to our landline telephone messages and picked up on a stranger's voice leaving a message to say: Saturday 11th March 7.38 pm: 'Oh hello. Good evening Mary. It's Lynne. You rang this morning and left me a message regarding Blondie. I'm just returning your call. I'm in this evening if you want to give me a call back.'

This, message, left the night before, was the sort which I might have ignored had I not heard a sharp double yap in the background, suggestive of puppy breeding activity. Moreover, my heart was racing from a particularly nasty and bitter tannin-tasting coffee I had bought from a Polish shop in the Uxbridge Road. An irresistible £1.30 for a bag of ground Arabica but I suspect that it may have been adulterated as it had a crack cocaine type kick to it. (Not that I would know what crack cocaine is like.) The doctor has banned me from having more than one coffee but I find it necessary to get me going in the mornings, to raise me, Lazarus-like, from the dead.

While Mary was sorting her bag upstairs, packing it ready to go up to London for another party, I made contact by telephone with my brother, sister and mother, to appraise them of this breaking news. I needed to prepare them for my possible imminent arrival as a houseguest if there is a showdown over the puppy. I even began to charge my mobile phone in anticipation of a long car journey. A Premier Inn would have been an extravagance beyond my wildest dreams if it came to a showdown.

I then telephoned the puppy breeder and left a fair but firm message in the style of Margaret Thatcher. (The urging to 'leave a brief message' always prompts me to ramble at great length.) I said that Mary was not in her right mind and consumed with grief and that accepting a new dog into a household required unanimity of resolve and purpose which was far from the case at the moment.

Blondie, from her portrait as shown to me by Mary, is an adorable puppy, for a fading Hollywood actress, but not for us at this point when our lives consist of rushing up to London for a ceaseless round of sixtieth birthday parties and leaving garden gates and doors open for Patrick the carpenter.

Moreover, presently there will be a field of lambs for Blondie to sink her teeth into. These always occupy the field opposite the cottage in spring. I can just imagine the headlines – '*Gogglebox* puppy shot in sheep worrying tragedy'.

'"I only looked away for a second," gasped a tear-stained Mary. "I was looking in my bag for my mobile."'

I could not have predicted that I would become so anti-dog since losing Phoebe the Tibetan Spaniel, but the scales fell from my eyes on an Anglesey beach at Aberffraw. On one side of the river was a procession of plodding glum dog owners being pulled along by their dogs. Damacene conversion against mutts came when I saw that, in reality, the dogs owned the humans and had enslaved them to the point of attaching them by string or rope

MARY: At the moment I'm too upset to comment.

Tuesday 14th

MARY: In the wake of Puppygate and feeling hostile towards Giles, I go to London to get sympathy from Gug One/Tintin, our first bed blocker.

Without wishing to downgrade now thirty-three-year-old Gug to the status of dog, he and Phoebe, our late Tibetan Spaniel, had a lot in common. They both served as highly-valued emotional props and now I've lost not only Phoebe but also Gug. He and his wife have decided to live in Florence for a year.

But he's in London for a week. Tonight is the only night we're both free.

We arrange to meet at fellow journalist's party in NW1 to launch his book on Brexit. Then we'll go to the Academy Club in Soho for a *tête-a-tête* over fishcakes.

The evening was a tragedy of errors. On the sensible grounds that we would be having our private bonding session later, Gug and I didn't bother talking to each other at the party.

At nine thirty, as the literary guests realised they had overstayed their welcome, there was a stampede to the door and, as the crowd thinned – or, as President Trump would have it of journalists, 'the swamp was drained' – our friends Cyril and Ursula came into focus.

'What are you two doing now?'

'We're going to the Academy Club.'

'Oooh, that sounds nice. Can we join you?'

Well, we like them very much so we said yes – knowing that as Cyril and Ursula used also to live in Wiltshire and are also maddened and delighted by Giles in equal measure, we could all enjoy discussing Puppygate.

But, since Gug had deleted his Uber app in Italy, we had to resort to a local minicab who needed directing all the way to Soho.

Wedged in the back with Cyril and Ursula while Gug directed the driver I couldn't talk to him. One hour later we were all still in the car. The London traffic was at its usual London standstill and Ursula announced, 'I've suddenly realised, Cyril, that you and I were in Russia this morning and I'm on antibiotics and I've been drinking, which I was told not to. I don't think I feel up to the Academy Club.'

They jumped out of the cab.

At last Gug and I could talk. But no, the driver even needed guiding from Tottenham Court Road to Lexington Street. It was ten thirty when we walked into the club to find it empty other than for five, four of whom we vaguely know.

'Pull up a chair,' they urged. And so, at one end of the table I talked to a former colleague for forty-five minutes while, at the other, Gug talked to her uncle who he'd never previously met.

'What a disaster!' we agreed as we settled into the black taxi taking us back. 'But at least we've got fifteen minutes now to chat... Did you give me back my debit card?'

'Yes. I definitely gave it back.'

For the rest of the journey I searched through my bagwoman bag looking for the card with a torch. As we pulled up at Gug's mother-in-law's he found it in his own wallet. 'I'm so sorry.'

'It's fine, but it's meant that for the last fifteen minutes we could have been chatting but instead I was bumbling through my bags. When are you off to Italy?'

'Tomorrow morning.'

When I got home the next day the tale elicited no sympathy from Giles who collected me from the station with an Annabel Grey oilcloth tablecloth taped to the rear windscreen of the Volvo. He refused to explain what had happened to the glass, as we drove home. Instead, he insisted that it was much more important that he got to the bottom of why I was 'gallivanting' in London in the first place, and in the second, why I had gone to the Academy Club for my private bonding session with Gug as I must have known we would know other people in there.

Worse, on entering the cottage I saw a clothes horse in the telly room festooned with ten socks and four shirts, and since I'd been away only one night, and the laundry basket was empty when I left, it was clearly another case of vexatious laundry. This time the outrage was compounded by what I call 'Gorbalisation' of the cottage, another of my trigger points.

Giles always feels happiest if he is fantasising about living in a butt and ben in the Gorbals and having to do laundry, eat and sleep all in the same room using the crackling log fire to heat it. He sees such a lifestyle as being ecologically correct because it allows him to efficiently husband the heat from the fire to help dry the clothes at the same time.

I don't share this fantasy.

It's always a mistake to confide your annoyances in your spouse to a female friend. Has anyone else noticed how many women seize on the confidence as a chance to be competitive over which has the least annoying husband? Such a friend often makes things worse (especially if she quite fancies him) by exaggerating Giles's deficiencies.

'It's all passive aggression,' emailed friend Zillah, 'because Giles has watched too many late night violent films on telly and, since he doesn't go out to work, and we humans NEED to interact with others to keep us sane, he has to save up all the aggression to download onto you as you walk through the door. And so while you're in London working, he portrays it as gallivanting, and then he does all this unnecessary laundry to signal that he's keeping the show on the road.

'Poor you. I do feel sorry for you. You don't deserve to be treated like this.'

GILES: It was an accident waiting to happen. Having designed my life as a stress-free zone, I'm not used to pressure and when it comes along, I tend to crumple under it.

Two separate events were on collision course. The first would be the epic appearance in our garden of a local man who, armed with crampons, harness and chainsaw, would be shinnying up a sixty-foot-high white poplar tree in my garden to eliminate it, lest it damage our garden hut – a nerve-wracking event for any landowner.

Moreover, the fellow had boasted that he wasn't insured. What if the brittle branches gave way under his weight? What if a neighbour from hell decided to videotape the spectacle for public consumption on YouTube? Poplar, after all, is known to be only good for matchsticks.

Meanwhile, a cavalcade of cars bearing the *Gogglebox* team was simultaneously heading down from London towards the cottage.

It had been originally timed so the two arrivals would be staggered but, in the event, Wiltshire men being time-fluid, and Mary having not kept me informed about the *Goggle* schedule before she went to London, the two parties became entangled and so did I.

First, two Land Rovers arrived: in one, the trusty Andy, my original chainsaw man, who had done his knee in, so ladder work was off the menu for him. In the second, the human monkey chum to whom Andy had subcontracted the felling work. Andy couldn't resist supervising it.

Their Land Rovers blocked off the field parking option for the *Gogglebox* team.

As I said to Mary, later, the accident wasn't my fault. The human monkey, who had already done a day's work and played a game of squash before he turned up to tackle my 60-foot tree, arrived late. But then one of the *Gogglebox* team arrived slightly early – in my book a sin worse than turning up late. It's a sin that poaches precious time that you thought you had to get ready.

Car parking spaces are at a premium in our village, and I quickly calculated that I could avoid a neighbour-from-hell situation by removing the outsize Volvo estate to a safe place, a field opening down the lane which serves as a passing place. It's interesting that most neighbour disputes kick off over car parking spaces or boundary fences. It demonstrates that man is a territorial creature, so Brexit is not such a mystery after all.

So, to pre-empt any such territorialism, I reversed the behemoth into the hitherto overlooked passing place. But so wrapped up was I in parking logistics and a radio play that, like an over-pressured air traffic control officer at Heathrow, I made a mistake. I reversed into the narrow space slowly and cautiously but failed to turn my head around to check the blind spot behind me. Unlike my overweight chum Danny whose neck is now so thick he cannot turn it at all and has to rely on a reverse parking in-car camera, I can turn my head partially. Yet I failed to do so and within the blind spot was a blackthorn twig which gently poked the rear windscreen out with a sickening splintering of glass fragments. The blackthorn is prized by walking stick makers for its durability and its vicious thorns which have been known to even puncture tractor tyres.

It turns out that so-called 'safety glass' as it's called, is also known as 'tempered glass', which means it's designed to shatter into thousands of separate glass pieces with the consistency of wet sugar, slush or melted snow. There I was trying to be helpful to make space for others... and the gods punished me. No good deed goes unpunished. On the other hand, compared to railway scenes at rush hour in Bangladesh my little incident doesn't even register.

Quite why I got my knickers in a twist is a mystery, since that morning I switched from two cups of caffeinated coffee to one caffeinated and one de-caffeinated coffee, as recommended by my German-born blood-pressure doctor.

But if Mary had seen the trouble I took to clear away the glass spicules – which cut my fingers twice (despite being called safety glass) – she might account for at least two hours of the day gone on 'own-goaling', as she calls self-inflicted and time-consuming accidents. I prefer to describe them, like the police do, not as accidents but as 'incidents', a term which implies that no one is to blame.

I hate broken glass: as a gardener I curse previous occupants who thought nothing of tossing jam-jars and perfume bottles over their hedges before the era of recycling. No doubt future generations will hate us for bequeathing them plastic bottles (viz, Henderson Island in the Pacific, the world's epicentre of plastic waste).

But, more worrying was the huge pile of broken glass on the edge of my bio-reserve. I didn't want to add to the problems of migrating frogs and can honestly say that I am the only villager, nay cottager, to have even heard of the major environmental problem dubbed the Global Declining Amphibian Phenomenon.

Thursday 16th

MARY: Giles kindly drove me to the high street of the local market town where I climb four storeys to the top floor of the White Horse Bookshop, the fountain of local civility, with its spectacular view over the, as yet, still not overdeveloped Downs. And then to the beauty parlour.

As a child I bitterly resented my mother's weekly visits to the hairdresser. The house was vault-like without her and, on her return, her hair always looked worse – lacquered, stiff and helmet-like. Yet she always seemed so animated post-these visits and inexplicably full of details of the hairdresser's drab life.

Now I myself have finally cottoned on to the joys of regular interaction with someone with whom you have nothing whatsoever in common, but with whom you have another sort of intimacy than what you have with friends or family.

Janine, the beautician, is someone who doesn't challenge me with Big Talk – only small. I prefer not to give her my own news – too stressy to think about. But I love listening to hers, about visiting her Mum in hospital, having a run-in with a parking warden, giving a client a full Brazilian wax when they only wanted the bikini wax.

'She said to me after, "I don't believe it. What have you gone and done? I only wanted a bikini wax."

'And I said, "You said a Brazilian."

'She says, "Yeah, but I meant a bikini. I thought you would've realised that."

'I said, "You must of felt me putting the wax on all over the area." And right back to the perineum, Mary, no way she couldn't have noticed.

'She said, "My partner's going to be livid about this."

'And I said to her, "Well, I can't put it back now. You make the best of it. Most ladies find they really like the feeling…"'

I'm thinking of my favourite female friends. None of them ever pampers me in a soothing manner while delivering an Alan Bennett-style talking heads monologue to which I can respond or ignore as I see fit. Indeed, most of my friends' conversation, now that I think about it, is around the subject of how much we have to do, and how inefficient are all the providers of services.

By contrast talking with – correction, listening to – Janine is so relaxing it's the conversational equivalent of the BBC Interlude films from our childhood showing a kitten playing with a ball of wool. The salon contains for me a parallel universe where blandness reigns and my only obligation is to unwind while Janine seems to be enjoying affixing the eyelashes.

And then I pay her and then we are all square. How often are you 'all square', metaphorically speaking, with a friend?

Monday 20th

GILES: Mary has presented to me the 'rest' diary she has been filling in on my behalf. Any day in which no cash was earned is now coloured in with high-vis marker pen and the words 'full day of rest' scrawled on top.

She believes the diary provides proof that I suffer from Work Dysmorphia in the same way as some people with low self-esteem about their perfectly good looks suffer from body dysmorphia, and that the ledger will help me to get a realistic view of how much work I actually did over the last year.

But I would dispute her definition of what work is. For example, waiting for workmen to turn up is a job in itself. It could be termed 'own work', an expression coined by fans of the 'citizen's income' – a scheme perennially suggested by alternative economists who wish to replace all state income, including benefits and pensions, with a standard issue weekly stipend for everyone. Those for whom the weekly stipend is not enough can then 'top up' with a separate income from gainful employment, without incurring penalties or stealth taxes.

I long for the weekly stipend to become a fact of life as I could then spend decades creating micro habitats for invertebrates and reptiles with a clear conscience that I was not ducking my responsibilities as a citizen to 'produce' or 'consume' or to be gainfully employed by brush or pen. Or indeed to feel the need to account for my hours in just standing and staring as recommended by the poet (and tramp) William Henry Davies:

> What is this life, if full of care,
> We have no time to stand and stare
>
> No time to stand beneath the boughs
> And stare as long as sheep or cows.
>
> No time to see, when woods we pass,
> Where squirrels hide their nuts in grass.
>
> No time to see, in broad daylight,
> Streams full of stars, like skies at night.
>
> No time to turn at Beauty's glance,
> And watch her feet, how they can dance.
>
> No time to wait till her mouth can
> Enrich that smile her eyes began.

A poor life this if, full of care,
We have no time to stand and stare.

This is surely a poem whose time has come.

Sunday 26th

GILES: I met a man at another wearisome sixtieth birthday party. If seventy is the new fifty, is sixty the new forty? I don't feel it, and nominal aphasia struck again. He greeted me with an enthusiasm which implied we were long lost friends but who on earth was he?

I caught Mary's eye and she moved forward to the rescue.

'Hello Pete. Do you know Blah Blah? Blah this is Pete Burrell who we met when we were staying with Sophy in Ireland... Pete's an agent. He represents Nigel Farage and Frankie Dettori...'

Mary stared meaningfully at me as she addressed Pete. 'Do you remember your idea for Giles's TV show?' she continued. "What the F*** Does Giles Do All Day?"

Then I remembered. Around fifteen years ago, when reality television was in its infancy, Burrell, who had stayed with us for a week in an Irish house party, made an outrageous suggestion. This was that I should wear a headcam in order to record my 'progress' through my day in a ground-breaking project which he dubbed 'What the F*** Does Giles Do All Day?' It would be a permanent channel into which followers could beam at any time of the day or night. It might win awards.

But I remember Pete saying that in order to make any inroads with the yoof of today, the f-word would be obligatory. It might be cult viewing or not and it would definitely dovetail into the emerging slow movement – slow food, slow cities etcetera – why not slow television? Years later the spectacle of stately progress from a fixed camera on a canal long boat along the length of the Kennet and Avon canal was shown to huge acclaim. Burrell's idea regarding creating a cult viewing platform featuring me was prescient.

With Dettori and Farrage under his belt, Burrell is clearly no amateur, but even were he to revive the idea now, Mary and I disapprove of swearing – especially on television. And so do 300,000 TV viewers who tuned off the Gordon Ramsay ITV *Nightly Show* debacle this week.

The new posh family of four *Gogglebox*ers in Dorset haven't sworn yet but I'm watching them like a hawk for lapses. The backlash against swearing has been evident for years as profanities, like a devalued currency, have by degrees lost their impact, although oddly not the c-word which still retains shock value. Colin Farrell famously used it in the cult film *In Bruges*, which I was not a great fan of.

I'm reminded that the late Alan Coren observed that, 'Television is more interesting than people. If it were not we should have people standing in the corner of our room.'

And I feel there may yet be a second career for me in the webcam arena if everything else falls through.

Noble work

Monday 27th

GILES: Invertebrates were on my mind today, and amphibians, when I spotted a hitherto unobserved tell-tale Hansel and Gretel snail trail of broken glass, the legacy of the windscreen mishap. It led from the layby to the field gate.

There is no CCTV in the village although I wish there had been today because I would like to have been caught on camera, for a 'slow telly' sleep-inducing hour's worth of my road sweeping with dust pan and brush.

It was bob-a-job man's work, as I explained to Mary, but none the less worthy for that – it was boring but important work. Noble work, indeed. Self-sacrificing.

'That's all very well but we can't really spare the time for you to be doing noble work. It was a pity you had to have the accident in the first place. It wasn't really self-sacrificing work. It was your fault, so you had to clear it up.'

'It was nobody's fault,' I replied calmly. 'Or rather, it was the fault of the projecting twig.'

Occasionally a really educational and worthwhile offering like *Restoration of the Year* comes up. Wasn't TV meant to be a tool for education? Mores the pity that the powers that be have not yet submitted it for review on *Gogglebox*.

The programme went to Bavaria to source authentic panes of 'period' glass for early nineteenth-century

Felton Park Greenhouse in Northumbria. This glass is made using traditional glassblowers' techniques unchanged since medieval times, and is consequently full of hand-blown ripples and imperfections. One of the most pleasing features of this 'imperfect' glass is the tiny champagne-like bubble of air trapped in the solid surface.

Brittle greenhouse glass used to be available to the householder for window glazing 'for less'. It dimpled and warped reality in a most pleasing and harmless way. Our cottage has such inferior panes in a few windows and herein is a clue to how I fritter many man-minutes away as the day proceeds.

By tilting my head this way and that I can turn the telegraph lines into a skipping rope; the cottage chimneys of the squat dwellings opposite swell into the size of small cars and tree branches get swallowed up in glass dimples like the gravitational pull of black holes only to flip back to normality at the slightest inclination of the head. Even the sheep can turn into grotesque monsters with practice.

No other cottager can achieve this legal high featuring a phantasmagoria of visual effects and distortions without recourse to hallucinogens or magic mushrooms. In the Seventies, we all read a book called *The Natural Mind* by Andrew Weil, proposing that man has always craved alternative states of mind; witness children in a playground spinning like whirling dervishes to make themselves dizzy. Yet modern safety glass in UPVC frames has ironed out imperfection and the charm of everyday domestic windows has gone to be replaced by a bland interface between the inside and outside world. So was the baby thrown out with the bathwater.

Health and safety has been the midwife to a lame new world of mediocrity and tamper-proof seals on milk cartons. Small wonder more and more folk are becoming depressed, it's modern life itself. Although I'm quite happy with today's relatively painless dentistry.

It seems every step of technological progress and subsequent legislation has involved the loss of charm or enchantment to some degree. Even jet bomber planes in the Fifties had considerably more élan and style than those of today. The sailing ships moored on the Thames gave contemporary writers of the nineteenth century the impression of 'a forest of masts'. Now? Nothing. The world of foreign travel is similarly prosaic in the extreme. A summer visit to Venice or Dubrovnik makes you feel as though you are in a zombie movie by George Romero.

Some kind of mathematical formula must be invented to formalise this equation of progress versus disenchantment. Let's call it Wood's Law. Fortunately, we have paintings and photographs to record the past, and how enchanting the gas street lighting of Leeds looked in the reflected puddles in the street paintings of Atkinson Grimshaw. There was a catastrophic loss of beauty when concrete replaced stone. I saw myself how this wrecked the hand-crafted integrity of stone-built houses in the much-maligned Tenerife in the Canary Islands. In order to see how beautiful these islands once were and how the architecture enhanced rather than degraded the scene you will have to visit the Marianne North permanent exhibition in Kew Gardens... Steam trains versus diesel and electric show the same steep decline in enchantment, and how cunning of J.K. Rowling to plunder this rich vein of nostalgia and wonderment of past technologies in the Harry Potter series.

One mile from our village there is an annual steam fayre, with rows of vintage tractors and paraphernalia dating even up to the 1950s. It is laid on by the Agricultural Preservation Society, which is the beating heart of Wiltshire. Nostalgia in its rejection of the present in general and of Intensive farming in particular, is not a negative emotion but a subversive rejection of the status quo: a form of latent energy waiting to be harnessed by some rabble-rousing contemporary version of William Cobbett.

The dead hand of banality is even creeping into country lanes, drowning out the sound of a spring chiff chaff as a reversing bin lorry bleeps its inane progress through its three-point turn.

What if we woke up tomorrow with collective amnesia following an earthquake where every pane of glass was shattered? It's an unlikely scenario, but supposing the recipe for making glass was lost?

We take so much for granted; I only know that sand and silica are part of the process and the Romans introduced the technology.

There is a strong counter-argument against self-sufficiency: part of the joy of living in a specialised, interdependent society is to let someone else worry about glass recipes and trade with them for cash.

Now soap is a different matter. Anyone can make it from wood ash and animal fats steeped in home-grown lavender essence. It's something I've wanted to try for years but have been too busy. Paper is not too hard to make either using basic materials or plant-derived materials but, again, I've been too busy to experiment.

I couldn't live in Wiltshire if I hadn't discovered the drastically under-read Victorian naturalist and novelist Richard Jefferies. He provides me with the enchantment that modern Wiltshire cannot.

The glass left by the ancients in their dwellings had long since been used up or broken, and the fragments that remained were too precious to be put in ordinary rooms. When larger pieces were discovered, they were taken for the palaces of the princes and even these were but sparingly supplied, so that the saying 'he has glass in his window' was equivalent to 'he belongs to the upper ranks'.

And later in the novel: 'The glass made now is not transparent, but merely translucent; it indeed admits light after a fashion, but it is thick and cannot be seen through.'

This is the sort of glass I would make if I turned glass maker. But what a shame you have to travel to Bavaria to obtain imperfect glass; there should be a campaign for 'real' glass. It is always up to us middle-class revivalists to set the trends. 'What did Giles do all day?' He gazed out of dodgy window panes, which cost him nothing but time, which is harmless enough unless you believe the despicable modern creed that time equals money!

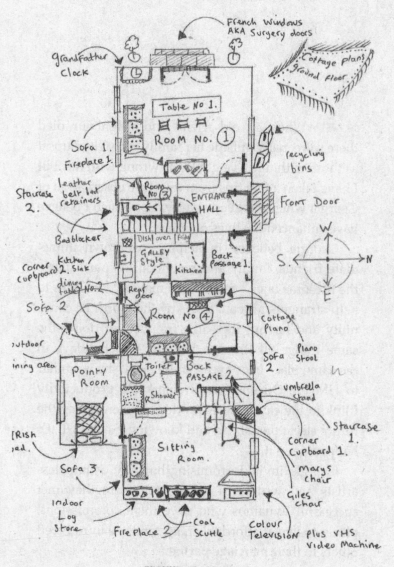

French Windows
AKA Surgery doors

Grandfather Clock

Cottage plans
Ground Floor

Table No. 1.

ROOM NO. ①

Sofa 1.

Fireplace 1.

recycling bins

Staircase 2.

leather belt bed retainers

Room No ③

ENTRANCE HALL

Front Door

Bedblocker

W

S.   N

Corner Cupboard 2.

Kitchen 2. Sink

Dish oven fridge

GALLEY Style

Kitchen

Back Passage 1.

E

dining table No. 2

Sofa 2

Rear door

Room No ④

Cottage Piano

Piano Stool

Sofa 2.

outdoor dining area

Pointy Room

Toilet

Back PASSAGE 2

umbrella Stand

Shower

Staircase 1.

[Irish bed.

bookshelf

Sitting Room.

Corner Cupboard 1.

Sofa 3.

Marys chair

Giles chair

Indoor Log Store

Fire Place 2

Coal Scuttle

Colour Television plus VHS Video Machine

GROUND FLOOR PLAN

233

POSTSCRIPT*

MARY: When an old friend and neighbour died there were many outside her family who felt as upset as those within it. I've got loads wrong with me, but I have taken a few tips from my close observation of Georgia when she lived nearby, tips which I believe have enhanced the lives of others.

Georgia believed in helping your own immediate friends, family and neighbours – particularly the tiresome ones – rather than making donations to help strangers abroad. She saw the worth of continuity and having the same friends and doing the same things all through her life: e.g., holidays in the same place every year. In this way she is similar to HM the Queen whose remarkable productivity I link to the calm that is produced when seeing the future stretching ahead and knowing exactly what's happening in it.

Georgia invited promising but lazy or hopeless artists and writers to her house where they met successful dynamos who gave them commissions, places to live at affordable rents, and she introduced others to their marriage partners.

She celebrated beauty instead of focussing on the negative and yet she kept an eagle eye on local newspapers and moved in to stop ugly developments.

She believed in 'compartmentalising'. She knew that, in the words of William Blake, 'Man was made for joy and woe' and once we accept that's the nature of life and stop taking the setbacks personally, 'Then through the world we safely go.'

Georgia's house, garden, vegetable garden, family and friends were perfectly maintained and yielding. She kept jobs, her figure and her husband in love with her.

But in a weird way it cheered me up to hear that, until after her death he hadn't realised 'how much she did'.

Giles and I are blessed by being members of the generation that can still use cultural and gender stereotypes without fearing someone snapping our heads off. It confirmed my theory that men in general – even men married to superwomen – have no idea how much their wives or partners do. It's not just the thankless tasks that are only noticed if we don't do them, we do all the emotional homework as well. We make the effort to go to the school sports day, prize-givings, end of term concerts; we make the children write thank you letters and clean their teeth; we hear out bores while they give us blow by blow accounts of things that have gone wrong because they clearly need to get them off their chest. We can't enjoy the anticipation of social events because our male partners can only say 'Do we have to go? I can't face it. Why can't people leave us alone? Let's just stay in and watch television.'

It's the not doing of these things that would cause everything to fall apart, but the doing of them goes virtually unnoticed and unappreciated.

But Georgia wouldn't carp on about it since she realised life was too short and it's clearly the human condition. And so I try not to. I want to celebrate the glorious and the positive and the laughs instead of wallowing in the negative and the nuisances.

Looking back on the year's diary I can see that one or two misunderstandings have been cleared up. I now understand why Giles wants to keep the kitchen sink in the state it's in – it's not sadism, after all, but an admirable attempt to buck the trend against built-in obsolescence. I've also just found out that his objection to Louise Brewer bringing us what he refers to as a 'threatening number of eggs' is not negorrhoea, but rather a dislike of having his 'cheese-paring cottage economy', as inspired by William Cobbett, suddenly distorted by a glut which makes him feel he is no longer the master of his own house.

Moreover, the kitchen gives pleasure to friends who can reassure themselves by saying 'At least our kitchen isn't as bad as the Woods.'

It has sunk in that he does cook three meals a day, light a log fire each night, and grow flowers and vege-tables (even if many of these turn out to be sacrificial crops as the pigeons and blackbirds get them first).

Using the voice memo on my iPhone and then typing up the arguments we have had I can often see that Giles had a point after all and I was being hysterical – but only because I was tired and had no time to listen.

GILES: It's astonishing how many nuisance appointments there are throughout the year. The worst things for me are things that are blocked in months ahead and are uncancellable. Fixtures, so to speak, in the diary, that hang over my life like the Sword of Damocles. I am glad I wrote the diary because now at least I know what I have done in one year of my life. I can remember being interviewed for *Wiltshire Life* magazine when I had an exhibition in the Mount House Gallery, Marlborough. The journalist asked me what I had been doing in the last ten years and I honestly hadn't a clue. I remember bellowing up the stairs to Mary, 'Apart from mending the windows, what have I done in the last ten years?' I did know that from 1988 to 1990 I successfully mended a few of the cottage windows using car body filler, and that I had searched for and made an assemblage of flints, arrowheads, scrapers etcetera from the Stone Age. The historian Paul Johnson once remarked that, 'usually talent comes allied with ambition but not in Giles's case'.

Looking back, I can see that when I won a music scholarship to Shrewsbury School it was entirely thanks to the pushing I received from my piano teacher Miss Anderson (Ma Andy) who kept me in over every break to practise like a Russian gymnast. It seemed at the time strict and cruel regime as the practising scales and arpeggios went on while other boys played outdoors. Once I got to Shrewsbury I never practicsed again.

Frequent kangaroo courts have taken place throughout my life with friends asking why I wasn't using my talent. The only person who has never criticised me is my mother who has always been amazed at how much I achieve on top of driving Mary around and doing the shopping as well as producing meals from an 'impossible' poky kitchen. 'You must be shattered' is her mantra. Mary thinks she has overpraised me and it is true that when I stay with her in Anglesey I am aware of this much-appreciated positive feedback – although it has to be said she even praises me for having done my teeth.

GILES'S SEVEN POINT PLAN FOR A STRONG AND STABLE MARRIAGE

1. Have parents who didn't split up. You are then statistically far less likely to do so yourself.
2. Think of the pastoral care. If, like the late John Noakes, I was found confused and sheltering in a storm drain in Majorca, I know Mary would strain every sinew to locate me.
3. Don't have unrealistic expectations. I believe too high a premium is set on the nebulous idea of personal happiness. Once this aspiration is removed, the marriage stands a better chance of not being derailed.
4. Because my brain cells are deteriorating more quickly than Mary's there's an obvious incentive to stay married to her. *Vide* Iris Murdoch and John Bayley.

5. Don't have a mistress. Luckily I don't have the income stream to meet the expectations for flowers and champagne a mistress would require.
6. Mary's memory bank. She can remember the details of stories and the points of them whereas I tend to tell the punchlines first without the build-up. I have become content to merely trigger Mary, like a human jukebox, to tell the relevant anecdote while I sit back. The temptation to tell the punchline two thirds of the way through still allows me to sabotage the occasional performance.
7. Finally – the mantra 'I've started so I'll finish', as heard on *Mastermind*, has always seemed to me a powerful bulwark against divorce.

MARY'S FIVE POINT PLAN FOR A STRONG AND STABLE MARRIAGE

1. Wear invisible wax earplugs while your partner is ranting on a familiar theme. You have heard it a thousand times before...
2. Keep different hours from the annoying partner so you have fewer waking hours exposed to them.
3. Give space in your home to a third person who can act as a buffer between you and your partner to make you all behave better.
4. Compliment your partner on his or her achievements and acts of kindness towards you.
5. Ignore their provocations.

GLOSSARY

BED BLOCKERS
Young people who come to help Mary and stay
overnight.

CRACKLER
A log fire.

ERASERHEAD
Means a living nightmare and links to the David
Lynch film.

FISH EYE

MARY: This is when Giles's eyes mysteriously
change shape from round to oval.

GILES: Mary links this to my consuming more than
one pint of beer. It may also be due to some local
environmental effect such as crop spraying. I am
obsessed by crop spray and the effect it is having on
me both mentally and physically. Never has a man

had so many body burdens. On top of the lack of minerals we then have to accommodate a cocktail of different chemicals either through direct inhalation or through food.

HATROLALLIA

MARY: This is when Giles says things he does not mean, just for effect. One terrible example was when he allowed a wonderful VW beetle to – allegedly – be scrapped just because it needed new brakes. The garage man, in Devon, said such parts could not be found. It was the days before mobiles so I couldn't ring anyone to check. 'You shouldn't throw good money after bad,' the garage man said. Giles said the same phrase about thirty times, even though he couldn't have meant it.

GILES: In my defence, I would say this. I spend so many hours on my own keeping the show on the road while Mary is gallivanting in London, I often simply enjoy the novelty of hearing my own voice and I make such remarks for want of anything else to say.

KICKOVER
A glass left on the floor so it gets kicked over and spilt or a dog's bowl not heavyweight enough to withstand kicking.

NEGORRHOEA

MARY: Giles complaining over everything including things that are good, e.g., 'Oh no! Don't say it's going to be good weather today when we could have done with it being good weather last Wednesday.'

PANDORA'S BOXING

MARY: This is when we are struggling to sort out one problem, but instead of concentrating on it, Giles tries to think of all the other problems we've got and mention them as well.

PETER PANNING

GILES: This is when I seize opportunities not to grow up. It was Peter Panning when I accepted an invitation to go on holiday with a couple of pensioners from the Vale of Pewsey who had a second home in La Palma on the Canary Islands. It was my last chance to sit in the back of the car and be driven to places like an overgrown child.

RATNERLALLIA

MARY: This is when Giles says something own-goalish, like when Gerald Ratner said the reason he could sell his products so cheaply was because they were basically all crap. Admirable though his honesty was, the upshot was that the Ratner jewellery empire collapsed and Gerald Ratner was deposed as chief executive. When Little, Brown wanted to commission Giles to write his first self-hinder book, Giles replied that there were already too many authors chasing too many readers.

Also 'Speculo-Pandora's Boxing', where Giles looks for all the problems we may have in the future.

SEANCEART

GILES: I can remember once channelling a bad artist as I tried to do art in bad taste. One of my first mosaic commissions was for a man who was the father of a former girlfriend from Harrow School of Art. I had seen from his own home that he had bad taste so I made the mistake of spending a year trying to produce a mosaic in bad taste instead of one I would enjoy looking at myself and which would come naturally.

SEANCESPEAK

MARY: When Giles channels someone else, rather than himself, and says what that person would have said in response to a situation.

SICKENER
A full English breakfast.

ACKNOWLEDGEMENTS

We would like to thank *Gogglebox*, Stephen Lambert, Tania Alexander and Chantal Boyle. Our agent Julian Alexander has been hands on, patient and encouraging. We are enormously grateful to Rachel Johnson and Ivo Dawnay, who have been key friends to us. Liz Marvin successfully juggled a massive, mental load while employing a forensic eye for inaccuracies and continuity as she read the text (as well as detecting hatrolallia).

We want to particularly thank Lorna Russell who had the idea for *The Diary* in the first place and, with her Olympian overview, steered the content from the splurges we submitted. If it is enjoyable and instructive to read, it's thanks to Lorna.